Sisters
FOREVER

OTHER BOOKS AND AUDIO BOOKS
BY MARILYNNE TODD LINFORD

Sisters in Zion

We Are Sisters

Sister to Sister

Sisters FOREVER

Inspiration for women

MARILYNNE TODD LINFORD

Covenant Communications, Inc.

Cover image *Birds Teal Background-Illustration* © Friztin.

Cover design copyright © 2014 by Covenant Communications, Inc.

Published by Covenant Communications, Inc.
American Fork, Utah

Printed in the United States of America
First Printing: March 2014

20 19 18 17 16 15 14 10 9 8 7 6 5 4 3 2 1

ISBN 978-1-62108-622-2

Table of Contents

Preface & Acknowledgments

EVERY MONTH FOR THE PAST thirteen years, I've written a one-page message for the sisters of my ward. It's been an unofficial calling from my Relief Society presidents—Sue Smith, Carol Pia, Carole Kirk, Kristine Philips, and Kathleen Miner. I thank them for encouraging me to continue. I enjoy writing these messages and pray the words benefit some sister in the ward. Several times, as new topics came to mind, thoughts flowed so simply and completely it was as though I were an observer watching the words appear without forethought or plan. Other times I struggled to meet the deadline of another month. All the so-so work is mine; everything filled with the Spirit came by the Spirit.

After *Sisters in Zion*, there came *We Are Sisters*, and then *Sister to Sister*. In the Salt Lake Temple, where Richard and I serve as ordinance workers, a fellow worker told me she had read the three books and suggested a title for the fourth one—*Sisters Forever*. I assured her there would not be another, but I was wrong. I thank Covenant for this bonus opportunity.

Thanks also to Betsy Nagel, a dear friend and talented editor, for her timely help with the manuscript. I thank Stacey Owen, my Covenant editor, who has the gift to make me look better than I am.

I thank my mother for her stability and contagious love. I'm thankful to my parents for giving me seven siblings. As the oldest of that tribe and a mother of eight, I've had the opportunity to quasi- or actually parent fifteen children. And, as expected, just when I think I finally get something right, a new mothering challenge appears. I'm grateful for our children and grandchildren, for their love and support, and for the good times we have together. I love my daughters-in-law and sons-in-law, who hopefully don't have too long of a list of scary mother-in-law stories to tell.

I'm grateful for my husband, who willingly edits everything I write. How I appreciate his creativity, love, and testimony. I'm thankful for my sisters, who are my dearest friends, and my friends who are like dear sisters. I am thankful to my sisters in the gospel with whom I've shared callings, visiting teaching, love, and friendship.

Sometimes I'm asked, "So what's your book about?" and, even though I've been asked that question since 2005 when *Sisters in Zion* was published, I still don't have a concise answer. It's really a very simple book of *short* chapters, averaging about the length of my attention span. There isn't a complicated plot or surprise ending. It's a book of unrelated topics without a specific theme. I hope you enjoy the variety. It's a book written specifically for women, ages 18 to 108.

It's a book about the cares, conflicts, disappointments, and pains of everyday life that are made better by living the gospel of Jesus Christ. (So I guess it really does have a theme.) I hope it's a book of hope, reflecting inner contentment, happiness, and pure testimony. I hope it's a book to help you transcend the routine, randomness, regrets, and rigors of the day. My prayer is that as you read, you will feel the Spirit testifying to your individual worth as a beloved daughter of your Father in Heaven.

*About the names used in this book: The people whose stories I tell have either given me permission to use their real names or their names have been changed.

Chapter 1

THE GIFT OF SISTERHOOD

IF YOU WERE PICKING TEAMS, you would choose Carla first because she's the kind of person who takes on your project as if it were her own. She is conscientious, radiates testimony, and is a true friend.

Carla began feeling extreme gratitude. Blessings in many areas of her life seemed to be tumbling in upon her family. She was especially grateful because her son, who was thirty-something and single, had recently married the girl of his dreams.

As she was basking in her season of gratitude, she began to feel heartache for some of her dear friends who were in seasons of trial. One had a daughter who had divorced an unfaithful husband. One had a son whose girlfriend had died. One had a four-year-old grandson suffering from heart failure. Another had two thirty-something children who desired marriage and family.

Carla felt sorry there was nothing she could do to help her friends. Then the Spirit whispered, "Pray for them," which sounds very ordinary, except the message was not to pray for her friends but for their sons and daughters by name. She said to one friend, "The inspiration I received that day to pray for your two children was direct and specific." Praying for each other's children by name is the gift of sisterhood at work.

Kathy saw Ann at the doctor's office. Ann suffers from chronic fatigue and accompanying depression. Kathy asked, "Are you coming to the ward party tonight?"

"No," said Ann. "But Barry will come with the children."

Kathy nodded, trying to be understanding but feeling perhaps it would be good for Ann to come. Kathy said a quick prayer that she could say something beneficial and then heard herself say, "You'll be missed."

When Ann walked in to the party with her family that evening, Kathy said a prayer of thanks. Praying for each other is sisterhood at work.

Megan saw Pam at the mall. She knew Pam had seen her but pretended not to. Megan felt she should say hello. When she got closer, she realized Pam had been crying. After the initial greetings, Megan asked Pam how she was coping with her husband being so ill. Pam answered with a question: "Do you have anything in life to look forward to?"

Megan said a quick prayer, feeling concern for Pam's emotional state, and asked, "Do *you* have anything to look forward to?"

Pam answered softly, "It would be nice," and turned her head away.

Megan went home and told her husband, who "just happened" to home teach Pam's family. With the bishop's help, he provided assistance at a crucial time. Acting on impressions is sisterhood at work.

Since all females are daughters of a loving Father in Heaven, we are truly sisters, which explains our instinctive feelings of sisterhood. Women of all races, cultures, and socioeconomic levels give in love. They cheer, help, and share naturally and freely as part of their divine nature. The Relief Society of the Church augments these natural tendencies and creates additional pathways of interconnectedness through visiting teaching.

A few years ago, my visiting teachers were both young mothers. On one visit, the lesson was about the blessings of motherhood. Within a few sentences, the young mother giving the lesson began to wipe away tears. *Hmm,* I wondered. *Can motherhood be this rewarding to her?* I knew she had a four-year-old son and a two-year-old daughter. When she really started to cry, I asked, "Is being a mother hard for you?"

She explained that motherhood didn't come naturally. She said, "I just don't have the skills or patience to be a mother." I asked for an example, and she described the four-year-old's abnormal behavior, with which I was familiar. I told her she was not a bad mother but that her son needed to be evaluated by a professional. Within a few days, she had been to the child's pediatrician, who referred her to a specialist. By Sunday, when I saw her again, she whispered that things were already getting a little better. She said she'd been praying for help. Doing your visiting teaching and welcoming your visiting teachers is sisterhood at work.

As daughters of God and sisters in the gospel, we watch over each other. We pray for each other, we pray for each other's children, we watch for opportunities to serve as prompted by the Holy Ghost. We freely share—giving and receiving—this precious gift of sisterhood.

Chapter 2

PLEASE OPEN MY EYES

A VERY NORMAL LATTER-DAY SAINT family, a father—Brian, a mother—Laura, and three boys ages ten, thirteen, and fifteen had a family home evening lesson centered on the idea that priesthood power is often evidenced when men who hold the priesthood follow promptings from the Holy Ghost to serve others and thereby become a direct answer to others' prayers.

This family was experiencing multiple levels of stress. Brian was recovering from heart surgery and couldn't work, and his mother was critically ill. She was being shuffled back and forth between the hospital and an extended care facility, and the outlook for her recovery looked bleak. One particular night, Brian, who was with his mother, called home to explain what was happening. Things weren't going well. He was exhausted but felt he shouldn't leave his mother's bedside.

Laura felt sad for her mother-in-law and for Brian, but things weren't going well at home either. It had been many months of chronic stress, and at this moment she felt like giving up and crawling into bed under the electric blanket. The boys' homework wasn't done, dinner dishes were piled on top of breakfast dishes, and nobody was ready for bed. Laura's frustrations boiled over as she yelled at the boys to go to bed. Then she escaped to the privacy of her bathroom to cry. Soon she was on her knees acknowledging to Heavenly Father that He was undoubtedly blessing them but that she couldn't see it. She prayed to have her eyes opened to His tender mercies.

She came out of the bathroom and barked more orders at the boys—then the doorbell rang. She hoped it wasn't anyone she would have to let in. Apprehensively, she opened the door and saw the full-time missionaries. She looked heavenward and thought, "Really? You sent me the missionaries?" It seemed such an inopportune time.

They said they were in the neighborhood and wanted to ask a few questions. Laura told them she was having a very bad day. They said they were sorry and wondered if they could share a song. She saw that the shorter missionary had what looked like a guitar case slung over his shoulder. So she invited them in, apologizing for the mess while clearing a space on the sofa, and called to the boys to come listen.

Soon the missionaries were singing "I Am a Child of God," and by the last verse, they were accompanied by Laura's audible sobbing. The Spirit reminded her of her pleading prayer only minutes before. She knew Heavenly Father always knows needs, but the timing and certainty of this experience revalidated her faith.

She said, "I invited them to have family prayer with us and thanked them for bringing the Spirit to our home. I also pointed out to the boys that through the power of the priesthood these missionaries had listened to the promptings of the Spirit to serve us as messengers of Jesus Christ." She wondered, "Of all the houses in our area, how could they come to our house, at this moment, carrying a guitar, with the desire to sing?"

Looking objectively at this snippet of life, we see what made this testimony-building moment possible for all involved.

This family holds family home evenings and teaches specific truths.

In this home, the priesthood of God is valued.

When this father is away, he calls home to keep his wife and children aware of where he is and how things are going.

This mother realizes when she's feeling depressed, and she humbly admits her weaknesses to and dependence upon Heavenly Father.

She has confidence in the power of prayer. She knows prayers are heard and answered. She, like Nephi, knows in whom she trusts. (See 2 Nephi 4:19, 23.)

She admits when she's having a hard time.

The guitar-carrying missionary learned how to play the guitar and brought it on his mission.

The missionaries know music brings the Spirit.

The missionaries follow promptings like Nephi. "And I was led by the Spirit, not knowing beforehand the things which I should do" (1 Nephi 4:6).

This mother doesn't let pride keep her from inviting the missionaries into her messy house.

When she opens her home to messengers of Jesus Christ, she opens the door to opportunities to be taught by the Spirit. She recognizes the answers to prayers and acknowledges the hand of God in her life.

Because of their mother's faithfulness, her sons are blessed to feel the Spirit and to see the power of righteous men.

This mother helps her sons identify this real-life tender mercy and reinforces the truths taught in the family home evening lesson.

Praying to have our eyes opened to see Heavenly Father's hand in our lives is a small, simple, and beautiful act of faith. Alma said, "By small and simple things are great things brought to pass" (Alma 37:6).

Chapter 3

Heavenly Father's Solutions Are . . .

USUALLY WHEN YOU ACKNOWLEDGE SOMEONE with "How are you?" it's just a greeting. You're not expecting a truthful answer. Neither is the typical reply honest but rather the automatic, "Good," which upon hearing, you nod, smile, and move on.

However, when you truly care about how the person is doing and say something like, "I know you're *good*, but how *are* you?" the sincerity in your voice may prompt an honest answer. It may be preceded by a long pause while the person weighs in her mind if she trusts you with the truth: "Well, honestly, I'm struggling right now," or "I'm just okay," or "I'm taking it a day at a time."

When you're struggling, just okay, or taking life a day at a time, it may be because you are pleading, begging that your Father in Heaven will grant you relief from the pains of life—a wayward child, a frightening medical diagnosis, a financial crisis, marital disharmony, a crisis of testimony. You feel intense sadness, and the constant churning in your brain, heart, and stomach won't stop.

Beth recently found herself in such a state of despair. Her prayers were a combination of weeping and begging: "Oh, whatever is going to become of us? Please, please provide a way out of this unbearable situation. I don't know how much more I can take."

Beth felt Heavenly Father had a Do Not Disturb sign on the door. Her knocking and petitioning seemed in vain, but she continued to cry, beg, and plead. Though she tried to pray in faith, hopeless and negative thoughts interrupted her concentration. When answers didn't come, she feared it was because she was unworthy.

One night in the midst of a turbulent prayer, a startling thought intruded: "What do you expect from me?" Beth stopped short and wondered, "What *do* I expect?" Was she really seeking a divine solution that would involve her dedicated best efforts, or did she want a genie that—*poof*—would make everything better?

Then she wondered about her approach to prayer. Were her pleading prayers actually complaining sessions? Was she acting like a drama queen? Was she speaking to the Master of the Universe with the attitude of a selfish child? Was she playing a celestial-type of Let's Make a Deal: "I'll be better at serving my neighbor (or whatever) if you will give me what I want now"?

What are your expectations from God your Eternal Father, who said, "I am God, and there is none like me" (Isaiah 46:9)? Of whom King David said, "Praise him for his mighty acts: praise him according to his excellent greatness" (Psalm 150:2). Who Helaman said has "miraculous and matchless power" (Helaman 4:25). Who Moroni said has "prepared a more excellent way" (Ether 12:11). Of whom we sing, "How wondrous and great Thy works, God of praise" (*Hymns*, no. 267).

Beth reviewed her prayers in her mind and realized she had done little thanking and praising, little remembering His blessings, and little acting in faith.

Then another thought came to her mind: "The Lord's solutions will be elegant."

Elegant. Elegant? Elegant! The word caught her off guard. After marveling at the communicated thought, she ended her prayer and looked up the meaning of *elegant*: graceful in appearance and behavior, ingenious, refined, dignified, cleverly simple, high-grade, splendid, majestic, classy, tasteful, excellent, superior.

She thought of things that are truly elegant—the power and beauties of nature, the human body, the plan of salvation. Then she recalled that one of Jesus Christ's names is the High Priest of Good Things to Come (see Hebrews 9:11). Then the scripture came to her mind: "Yet shew I unto you a more excellent way" (1 Corinthians 12:31).

Ideas tumbled in upon her. The gift of the Holy Ghost is elegant. The principle of agency is elegant; the Fall, the Atonement, the Resurrection, prayer, prophets, scriptures, priesthood, repentance, forgiveness, baptism, the sacrament, the Sabbath day, temples, family, babies, children, missionaries—all are elegant.

Beth's daily prayers became opportunities to praise and thank Heavenly Father for His elegance. In her daily scripture study, she found elegance on nearly every page. She began to notice elegance in family members, friends, and strangers.

Our all-knowing, all-wise, all-loving Father is the author of elegance, as Psalm 30 testifies: "I cried unto thee, and thou hast healed me. . . . Weeping may endure for a night, but joy cometh in the morning. . . . Thou hast turned for me my mourning into dancing" (30:2, 5, 11). Is not being healed elegant? Is not weeping that becomes joy elegant? Is not mourning that turns into dancing elegant? His gifts are elegant because they are eternal.

When you're struggling, Heavenly Father's understanding of and compassion for your situation is real. His plan for you *is* elegant. He will enable you to be better and to be equal to whatever challenges you face.

Anticipate good things to come from "the high priest of good things to come." So much so that in the not-too-distant future when someone asks, "How are you?" you will answer with reverent awe, "Heavenly Father is doing elegant things in my life."

Chapter 4

IN-BETWEEN TIMES

A SPACE OF TIME EXISTS between finding out about a problem and resolving it. A problem could last seconds, years, or a lifetime. However long it is, the time in which you don't know how things are going to turn out is the only time you can actively evidence your faith. Before the problem comes, you can't exercise your faith in a positive resolution because the problem doesn't exist or at least you don't know about it yet. After resolution, you can't exercise your faith because you have knowledge of how the conflict was resolved. The test is what you do during the in-between time while the problem, the trial, or adversity is happening.

Birth and death are exact starts and stops. Receiving an invitation to speak in church begins with receiving the assignment and ends with the "amening" at the close of the talk. The starts and stops, beginnings and endings, are not nearly as important as what transpires in between.

A father sends two sons on an errand. They both go. The in-between time starts ticking. The task is difficult. One son gives up, saying the job is too hard. The other son keeps working until he accomplishes the task. Both sons begin their in-between time with their father's request; both end when they report to their father. How they used the in-between time makes all the difference.

Two women desire a vegetable garden. They both go to the store and purchase seeds. The in-between time begins. One woman reads the back of a seed packet, realizes how much work is involved in growing a garden, and decides it's not worth it. The other woman reads the back of the seed packets, prepares the soil, plants the seeds, waters, fertilizes, thins, and weeds and weeds. In a few months, the in-between time ends, and the harvesting, eating, and enjoying begin—but only for the one who used the in-between time to plant and care for seedlings.

Alma 32 teaches how faith is active in the in-between times and dormant—asleep or inactive—in the befores and afters. This is the rhythm: A problem presents itself. You activate your faith specific to the needs and challenges of the problem. You faithfully work until the problem is resolved. Your faith goes into a dormant stage for that situation because it is resolved.

If problems and troubles came one at a time, the pattern would be easier to see, but you and I juggle dozens of situations simultaneously, and it's hard to keep faith active on many battlefields at the same time. It's hard to resist the temptation to throw up our arms in despair or run away saying it is too hard or takes too much time and energy or maybe even wanting to "curse God and die," which is what Job's wife suggested he should do during his most dire moments (see Job 2:9).

Sustaining faith through the in-betweens takes energy and determination to stay focused. Sustaining faith through trials takes a form of work called prayer (Bible Dictionary, "Prayer"). Sustaining faith takes sensitive hearing to still and small promptings from the Holy Ghost. Sustaining faith is increased through priesthood blessings. I heard a man testify at the conclusion of a horrific and very public adversity, "I survived priesthood blessing to priesthood blessing."

After my doctor told me my hair was going to fall out due to chemotherapy, I went wig shopping. I tried on many different colors, lengths, and styles. Finally, I decided to buy one that was most like my natural hair. I went to the cash register to pay for it, never imagining that one of the most significant moments of my breast cancer experience—perhaps of my life—was about to occur. I watched the owner of the shop write a word on the receipt.

"What did you write?" I asked, pointing to the word.

"I wrote the name of your wig," the clerk answered.

"Wigs have names?" I asked.

"Yes. Most have women's names," the clerk explained.

"What's my wig's name?" I asked.

"Faith," she answered.

Oh! It's a message from heaven, I thought. *I will walk in Faith, talk in Faith, pray in Faith; control my fearful thoughts in Faith, do and be in Faith, and, God willing, get well in Faith.*

Wearing "faith" gets us through the in-between times, through the starts and stops of adversities.

Chapter 5

DID ANYTHING OF IMPORTANCE HAPPEN TODAY?

ACCORDING TO APOCRYPHAL HISTORY, KING George III made a note on the evening of July 4, 1776: "Nothing of importance happened today." Who knows whether or not he actually wrote those words on that momentous day when fifty-six courageous men committed high treason by signing the Declaration of Independence? Mothers often feel and think those thoughts at the end of any number of busy, stressful, complicated days.

Months before it's official, the soon-to-be mother endures morning, evening, or all-day sickness. She submits to undignified procedures of poking and prodding and watches her figure morph. Baby kicks at her ribs, sits on her bladder, and saps her energy. She plans, prepares, and forgets there is any other topic of conversation, and drops into bed each night hoping something of importance happened today.

On the day of a baby's birth, a mother survives labor and delivery or the agony of waiting and the anticipation of adoption. When baby is placed on her tummy or in her arms, she thinks "I'm a mother!" and gazes at the new little face, watching one breath follow another. Truly something of wonder happened today!

As the days turn to weeks, the feedings seem constant. Days and nights blur. Her depleted energy quotient dips lower, and postpartum blues may surface. She bathes tiny feet, and laundry doubles. She endures colicky evenings and sleeps with one ear open in order to answer tiny cries. In blissful moments, mother and baby cuddle and rock together because, even though she's new at this, she senses these moments are fleeting. She will change diapers approximately 5 times a day, 365 days a year for at least 2 years—or 3,650 times. As the excitement of motherhood becomes routine, she wonders if anything of any importance happened today.

She plays peek-a-boo and sings "I Am a Child of God." Then it happens. She thinks she sees a smile! She makes notes in the baby book and posts photos on her blog. She watches baby roll over, reach, sit, stand, climb, walk, stumble, and fall. The first few times, she picks him up and coddles him. Soon, however, she lets him pick himself up, giving him encouragement and praise from the sidelines.

As bedtimes come, she reads the same words her mother read to her and her grandmother read to her mother—"In the great green room there was a telephone and a red balloon and a picture of the cow jumping over the moon"[1]—and drops off to sleep with her little one, hoping something of importance happened today.

When sickness comes she is the spoonful of sugar that helps the medicine go down. When nightmares come she rubs the little back and whispers comforting words. Too soon two candles burn on the birthday cake, and she suspects baby number two is on the way. She wonders: "Can I do it again? Can I love another as much?" Feeling overwhelmed and realizing she may never get enough sleep again, she looks heavenward to ask: "Is something of importance happening here?"

Birthdays keep coming, and soon there are three children in her care. Some days she washes her hands at least fifty times between changing diapers, wiping noses, and preparing endless meals—where the last meal is not fully cleared away before the next one is in process. If anyone is counting, she prepares 3 meals a day, 365 days, for about 20 years—or 21,900 meals—to raise three little ones.

She plays the same games and reads the same books ad infinitum. She knows what to say when a bad grade shows up on a report card. She wipes away tears, saying, "I'm sorry. You can do it, and I will help you." She listens to practicing, watches swim lessons, attends games and recitals, and becomes taxi driver and in-house doctor and nurse. She speaks her love, expresses affection, and hopes she is meeting needs. Her workload increases as emotional challenges amplify. Above the noise and commotion of goings and comings, she hopes that a little something of importance is happening.

She reads scriptures, prepares family home evenings, and drives to early morning seminary. She celebrates successes, little and big, and empathizes when adversities come. Her roles become more

---

1 Margaret Wise Brown and Clement Hurd, *Goodnight Moon*, New York: Harper-Collins, 1991.

challenging—resident philosopher, psychologist, and philanthropist. She teaches the value of money, hard work, budgeting, saving, and tithing. She exemplifies charity, helping children think of others' needs. She teaches organization and goal setting; she challenges each child to do his or her best and to reach for potential. She instills principals of integrity, saying, "Right is right even if nobody is doing it, and wrong is wrong even if everybody is doing it." She models a positive attitude. She laughs and cries and prays and prays and prays. She attends the temple and prays some more, trusting that something of importance is in progress.

In the briefest of moments, she's writing letters to missionaries, planning weddings, and welcoming grandchildren; yet the question may linger: "Was it worth it? Did anything of importance happen today?" And the Spirit assures, "Yes, on this day and so many others."

Joseph Smith discovered, "It was clearly evident that the Lord gave us power in proportion to the work to be done, and strength according to the race set before us, and grace and help as our needs required" (*HC* 1:176). So it is with motherhood.

Chapter 6

BIRTHRATES AND BABIES

IN 1798, THOMAS ROBERT MALTHUS published *Essay on the Principle of Population*, espousing his thesis that populations grow exponentially while food production grows geometrically. To avoid the catastrophe of extinction due to famine, Malthus urged controls on population.

Dr. Paul Ehrlich, in 1968, repeated what Malthus had theorized. In *The Population Bomb*, Ehrlich began:

> The battle to feed all of humanity is over. In the 1970s the world will undergo famines—hundreds of millions of people are going to starve to death in spite of any crash programs embarked upon now. At this late date nothing can prevent a substantial increase in the world death rate, although many lives could be saved through dramatic programs to 'stretch' the carrying capacity of the earth by increasing food production. But these programs will only provide a stay of execution unless they are accompanied by determined and successful efforts at population control.[2]

Nations and individuals responded as though Ehrlich's words were gospel truth. Obviously, today, we know he was a prophet of doom rather than truth. Not only did his predictions fail, but the exact opposite is occurring.

The Demographic Winter is a two-part documentary on population growth. You can watch it at youtube.com/watch?v=lZeyYIsGdAA. As you read the following statistics, keep in mind that the replacement fertility rate is 2.13 babies per couple. You would think the population would replace itself if two parents had two children, or a 2.0 replacement

2 Paul R. Eirlich, *The Population Bomb*, Touchstone Books, 1991.

fertility rate. But factors such as couples who cannot have children, the age of couples when their children are born, and deaths of infants, children, and teens, bring the replacement birthrate to 2.13.

1. Fertility rates have declined 50 percent in the last 50 years.

2. Ninety countries and territories have sub-replacement fertility rates. For example: Poland, Greece, Latvia, Romania, Spain, Italy, Germany, Japan are all at 1.3. Currently, in Russia, there are 140 deaths for every 100 births.

3. If the trend is not reversed, a child born in those countries will likely have few if any siblings or cousins and will have to care for two aging parents and four elderly grandparents.

4. The world's population will decline in the lifetime of today's youth.

5. This decline will have unexpected consequences. Gross domestic product cannot increase without sufficient workers in the working-age population, ages 16–64.

6. The U.S. government cannot continue social security. Today, it takes three workers to support one retiree. When the number of workers decreases, the system is unsustainable. The same is true with health care—too many old, too few young.

Statistics look backward, measuring the past and identifying trends. Prophecy, the word of God to His prophets, helps the faithful live today as well as prepare for the future. Trusting God is the wisest, safest course. So, how does God view the population issue?

In the beginning, He commanded Adam and Eve to multiply and replenish the earth (see Genesis 1:28). This commandment is still in force today. It has not been rescinded or modified. It is the crowning honor and blessing of husband and wife to have children.[3]

God numbers His children and knows what it takes to feed and shelter them. He said, "For the earth is full, and there is enough and to spare; yea, I prepared all things, and have given unto the children of men to be agents unto themselves" (D&C 104:17). He has prepared all things, there is enough and to spare, and men and women are responsible as His agents to judiciously use the earth's resources. In 1909, F. M. Bareham, who understood these principles, wrote about crucial life priorities:

---

3 See Neil L. Anderson, "Children," http://www.lds.org/general-conference/2011/10/children.

A century ago men were following with bated breath the march of Napoleon and waiting with feverish impatience for news of the wars. And all the while in their homes babies were being born. But who could think about babies? Everybody was thinking about battles.

In one year between Trafalgar and Waterloo there stole into the world a host of heroes: Gladstone was born in Liverpool; Tennyson at the Somersby Rectory; and Oliver Wendell Holmes in Massachusetts. Abraham Lincoln was born in Kentucky, and music was enriched by the advent of Felix Mendelssohn in Hamburg.

But nobody thought of babies, everybody was thinking of battles. Yet which of the battles of 1809 mattered more than the babies of 1809? We fancy God can manage His world only with great battalions, when all the time he is doing it with beautiful babies.

When a wrong wants righting, or a truth wants preaching, or a continent wants discovering, God sends a baby into the world to do it.[4]

We understand what is expected of us. We welcome and treasure babies and children in our lives. "Lo, children are an heritage of the Lord: and the fruit of the womb is his reward" (Psalm 127:3). The scare tactics of the world regarding overpopulation are just that. We know Heavenly Father would not plan for and direct the creation of an earth that could not sustain the spirits assigned to live there. However, we are expected, even required, to be good stewards. Through His grace, under the influence of the Holy Ghost, and as we keep His commandments, ideas and solutions will come without drumroll or fanfare. Watch and marvel at His magnificent ways as future prophets, political leaders, and problem-solvers quietly come to earth to homes like yours.

---

4 As quoted in Spencer W. Kimball, *Faith Precedes the Miracle*, Salt Lake City: Shadow Mountain, 1972, 323.

Chapter 7

HOLD ON

LATE ON A SATURDAY NIGHT, Jill's friends read her Facebook post: "*People are so mean, so cruel and heartless. I'm tired of being strong, of fighting. Life is too hard. I don't understand. The devil is too strong.*" Friends responded quickly: "*You're loved more than you think.*" "*No matter how bleak this moment seems, it will not last.*" "*Let's chat.*" "*Hold on.*"

Depression, heartache, and despair have been the common lot of humankind since Adam and Eve lost Eden. Life has not been easy in any generation, not for any family, not for any individual. How painful to watch birthdays accumulate without the desired marriage. Oh the aching for motherhood that goes unfulfilled month after month, year after year. How wrentching the abandonment felt by the widow and divorcee. How gnawing the unquenchable yearning for the prodigal son or daughter who has not yet returned.

King David wrote, "Trouble and anguish have taken hold on me" (Psalm 119:143). Alma wrote, "Satan has great hold on [their] hearts" (Alma 27:12). Joseph Smith asked God where He was hiding: "O God, where art thou? And where is the pavilion that covereth thy hiding place?" (D&C 121:1). No doubt Jill has asked that question.

Sometimes it does feel like God is hiding and the devil is too strong. In her hour of desperate aloneness, Jill reached out. What else can you do when there is no fight left in you, when you feel you are losing not a skirmish but the war?

Nehemiah, of the tribe of Judah, was born during the Babylonian captivity. He and his people were slaves and longed for the day they could return to Jerusalem. Since Nehemiah had never seen Jerusalem, he asked older friends and family what it was like. They told him wonderful stories about the great walled city and beautiful temple. His paramount desire was to see Jerusalem for himself.

Nehemiah served King Artaxerxes as a cupbearer. In this responsibility, he protected the king from being poisoned by his enemies. If Artaxerxes's food or drink contained poison, it would be Nehemiah who would die, not the king. As risky as the cupbearer's job was, it gave Nehemiah a presence in the king's court.

One day Nehemiah asked some of his brothers what they knew about a group of Jews who had escaped from Babylon and returned to Jerusalem. They sadly reported that the group was "in great affliction and reproach: the wall of Jerusalem also is broken down, and the gates thereof are burned with fire" (Nehemiah 1:3).

At this news, Nehemiah wept and mourned. If he'd had a Facebook page, his post may have read much like Jill's: *"I am a slave in a foreign land who risks being poisoned daily. I have no conceivable way to better my circumstance. My homeland is broken down, my people in bondage. I'm tired of being strong. Life is too hard."*

For Nehemiah, the hopelessness of his situation drove him to seek God in fasting and mighty prayer, yet sadness showed on his face. One day, the king asked him why he wasn't his normal, cheerful self. Nehemiah replied that his sadness was because of the condition of Jerusalem, specifically the walls and gates. Shockingly, the king asked how he could help. (Kings don't usually care about their slaves.) Nehemiah boldly asked for permission to go to Jerusalem. Artaxerxes gave him a letter of authority to return to Jerusalem to repair the wall and gates and even appointed him governor of Jerusalem.

In *The Secret Garden* musical, Martha sings to Mary, "Hold On." The song presents in three vignettes different adversities: a swirling storm, a paralyzing nightmare, and a face-to-face meeting with evil. Basically, Martha's message to Mary is, "Continue the good you're doing, and hold on because you can outlast the adversity. It's the storm, the nightmare, the evil that will go away, not you!"[5]

Holding on is evidence of hope. Holding on is what you can do when there's nothing else. Holding on is what Lehi, Sariah, Sam, and Nephi did through the dreary wilderness, the mist of darkness, the murk of the filthy river, and the ridicule of mockers in the great and spacious building. They held on to the rod of iron. "Hold on" is what the Lord told Joseph Smith to do. "Therefore, hold on thy way" (D&C 122:9). And you just keep holding on because life keeps coming at you.

---

5 "Hold On," ST Lyrics, http://www.stlyrics.com/lyrics/thesecretgarden/holdon.htm.

In Nehemiah's case, getting to Jerusalem was the easy part. Three men—Sanballat, Tobiah, and Geshem—conspired with fellow Arabians, Ammonites, and Ashdodites to keep Nehemiah's people from rebuilding the wall. Nehemiah armed his workers and assigned watchmen to guard the wall day and night. Nehemiah knew his enemies "thought to do [him] mischief," so he refused to meet with them, saying, "I am doing a great work, so that I cannot come down: why should the work cease, whilst I leave it, and come down to you?" (Nehemiah 6:2–3). Despite these major adversities, Nehemiah and his people held on and finished the wall in fifty-two days!

Challenges and adversities continue like hailstorms in your face, but solutions come as sweet, tender-mercy embraces—a friend, an idea, an unexpected bonus, a medication, a blessing, a priesthood leader, a scripture, a reconciliation, a tangible answer to prayer, courage to grasp and hang on to the iron rod. The rescue of Nehemiah is a type. Your rescue and Jill's rescue will come. Hold on.

Chapter 8

ANGELS WILL ATTEND YOU

MARIA WROTE:

For the past week or so I've experienced some serious depression. During work I managed to put on my game face, but the moment I was no longer on duty, I could repress the feelings no more. Like most people, I generally avoid painful things, so instead of dealing with the stuff that was really going on, I focused on more trivial stuff, like losing my wallet.

I'm involved in a difficult process of healing and growth too, so allowing space for those feelings, and those hours of tears . . . well, that's just part of the journey of healing from years of abuse. My therapist told me there would be an end to the tears at some point, and to let them come. So I did, most of Saturday night until near dawn. But in those hours when it felt like I was an island of one, I knew I wasn't alone. Though I felt lonely and was in intense emotional pain, when it was hard to ask God for help out of fear of not getting it, He helped me anyway.

First, I forced myself to go to the grocery store shortly before it closed Saturday night and ran into a woman from my church. Our chat was the reason I made myself go to church the next day when I was strongly tempted to justify not going.

Then my husband spent some time talking to me, even though he had to get up in five hours and pull a thirty-plus-hour shift. He helped me to keep perspective and hang in there through this process. He helped remind me that depression is an illness and that I am just sick right now, like having the flu or any other thing. It will pass, and I'm doing what I need to do to heal.

Then in the wee hours of the morning, a beloved friend, my maid of honor at my wedding, who I have had only intermittent contact with over the past nineteen years sent me an e-mail in the throes of my long dark night, to tell me I was on her mind and she just wanted me to know how much she loves me. And then another friend sent me a link to a great talk, which I read before finally going to sleep.

In the morning, I even got myself to church, albeit wearing sunglasses to disguise my puffy eyes. When sacrament meeting was over, a friend sought me out and invited me to walk with her to her house to take some rolls out to rise. She lives very close, so it didn't take long, and we attended the rest of our services together. After church another friend called who had seen me from a distance but hadn't had the chance to say hi, just to see how I'm doing.

These tender mercies were, I know, my Heavenly Father's way of reaching me, when I was too numb to feel much at all. And it occurred to me that He knew the whole time that my wallet was not stolen or lost. He knew all weekend that I would make it through this round of intense anguish. And He showed me His love by inspiring people to connect with me. (Used with permission)

Claudia, who has suffered through two divorces and through losing two husbands to death—one to a heart attack and the other to suicide—felt alone, so terribly alone and forgotten. To further complicate her life, she was in a terrible accident. After she was released from the hospital, her Relief Society sisters visited, helped, and comforted day after day for several months. When she was mostly recovered, she wrote a thank-you note to her Relief Society president that read, "You sisters have taught me so much by your service. When I am better, I'm going to find others to serve as you have served me."

When she had enough strength, she felt a renewed interest in the temple and asked a fellow widow if she'd like to go with her. They even took a couple of trips to other temples. Then she started visiting a woman who was dying of leukemia. When this woman passed away, Claudia started visiting an elderly woman, holding family home evening every Monday night with her. When this woman died, Claudia started visiting another elderly woman in the ward. Then she began reading the scriptures and found understanding she'd not found before. As these circumstances began to line up in her mind, she knew a loving Heavenly Father had blessed her to become involved in serving others. Bearing her testimony one fast Sunday, she said, "I guess I haven't been as alone as I thought I was."

These women are not unlike each of us. We can be alone in a crowded store, a packed chapel, or a houseful of people. In your lonely times, when you feel forgotten, when you feel like crying out to God even as our Redeemer pled, "If thou be willing, remove this cup from me" (Luke 22:42), be aware and attentive to the feelings, thoughts, and actions of others in the "thens," "afters," "whens" and "in the mornings." In these moments you will receive evidences of divine attentiveness, and it will often come through women in your life.

Watch as family members, friends, and even strangers are stationed, as if by assignment, in a grocery store aisle where you happen to be, send you a Facebook greeting, e-mail you a talk or thought just when you need it, or help and mourn with you in your most helpless moments after an accident or death of a loved one. Both heavenly unseen angels and mortal angels will be near you and attend to your needs. You are not as alone as you think you are.

Chapter 9

WHAT HOLDS FAMILIES TOGETHER?

IN THE 1990s, DR. MARSHALL Duke of Emory University and Bruce Feiler, a *New York Times* columnist, discussed the antifamily forces causing the "dissipation of the family" and what could be done to "counteract those forces." Since that time, they and others have discovered "a surprising theme." Mr. Feiler recently introduced these findings to his readers by asking, "What is the secret sauce that holds a family together?" and "What are the ingredients that make some families effective, resilient, and happy?"[6]

His answer: "Develop a strong family narrative." Okay, but what is a "family narrative"? Simply put, your family narrative is your family's story. The whos, whats, whens, wheres, whys, and hows of your family.

Mr. Feiler explained an interesting series of events. Sara Duke, Dr. Duke's wife, was a psychologist who worked with learning-disabled children. In her work, she noticed that the "ones who know a lot about their families tend to do better when facing challenges." She told her husband about her observation, and he told one of his colleagues, Robyn Fivush. Together they developed a twenty-question test to measure how much a child knew about his or her family.

In 2001, after compiling the list, they surveyed the children, also taping their dinner-table conversations. The research team compared these results to other psychological tests given to the children. The results validated the theory. "The more children knew about their family's history, the stronger their sense of control over their lives, the higher their self-esteem, and the more successfully they believed their families functioned."

The test became the "Do You Know?" (DYK) scale and "turned out to be the single best predictor of children's emotional health and happiness."

---

6 Bruce Feiler, "The Stories That Bind Us," *New York Times*, April 2013.

Drs. Duke and Fivush did not know that a couple of months later on September 11, 2001, terrorists would attack the United States and their thesis would again be validated. After 9/11, they retested the children, and "once again," Dr. Duke said, "the ones who knew more about their families proved to be more resilient, meaning they could moderate the effects of stress," as small as a sliver or as major as an act of war close to home.

The most wonderful aspect of this research is that every parent can apply it. By sharing details about their families, parents give their children an important set of skills. It costs nothing, and the return on investment benefits the entire population. Adding another confident, secure, and emotionally healthy citizen to the world enriches everyone and everything. This simple process gives the child self-confidence as well as what Dr. Duke calls "an intergenerational self. They know they belong to something bigger than themselves."

The study also shows that it doesn't matter what happened in the family because the lesson is that every family has ups and downs. Good and bad happen to everyone. Whether Grandpa was rich or poor, educated or not, made wise or foolish choices, our family came through it. Even when the house burned down or Aunt Ethyl got run over by a train or Papa lost his job, we got through it. That's what families do; they get through stuff together. This feeling of "family" becomes a person's core identity.

The U.S. military has likewise found that helping recruits feel a sense of unit identity "increases camaraderie and ability to bond more closely with their unit. . . . Until recently, the military taught unit cohesion by 'dehumanizing' individuals." The stereotype of the drill sergeant who bullies cadets does not happen as much anymore. Present training at the Naval Academy has "graduating seniors . . . take incoming freshmen (or plebes) on history-building exercises, like going to the cemetery to pay tribute to the first naval aviator or visiting the original B-1 aircraft on display on campus."

Dr. Duke wrote that it is interesting to note who in the family transmits this family information.[7] More often than not, mothers and grandmothers pass on this information. When and where do they share the family narrative? It is "passed during family dinners, family vacations, family holidays."

---

7 M. P. Duke, A. Lazarus, and R. Fivush, "Knowledge of Family History as a Clinically Useful Index of Psychological Well-Being and Prognosis: A Brief Report," *Psychotherapy: Theory, Research, Practice, Training*, 45, no. 2 (2008): 268–72.

Dr. Duke cautions, however, that just knowing the answers to the twenty questions doesn't *guarantee* higher self-esteem, lower anxiety, or completely resolve behavioral problems. But, he believes, "Knowledge of family history reflects certain processes that exist in families whose members know their histories."8

Beyond just knowing about their shared history, families bond through multigenerational activities. Parents should also establish traditions for holidays, vacations, and celebrating milestones. It doesn't seem to matter what the tradition is, only that it happens. Traditions contribute to a child's core identity.

All the above is true but comes with a caution. The family talk that builds strong families is a narrative. It is not gossipy or spiteful, sarcastic or angry. It does not continue the feud between the Capulets and the Montagues, but it may include the facts that Great-Grandpa got married and divorced four times or that Uncle Edgar spent significant time in the county pokey. It is the reality, the facts, not a Pollyanna-ish whitewashing nor intergenerational blame or anger.

If the tone of the narrative is negative and the theme is "nothing ever works out for our family," that is what will continue in the future. If the tone is positive and the theme is "yes, bad things did happen, but we have the ability to bounce back," that is what will continue in the future. Share the stories but not the garbage. These narratives boost unity and pride not because nothing ever went wrong but because our family can work through problems. Our family can do hard things.

It is interesting to think of the Bible and the Book of Mormon as a collection of family narratives that have become backbone examples to many. Opening to the first words in the Book of Mormon is a fine example of a family narrative.

"I, Nephi, having been born of goodly parents, therefore I was taught somewhat in all the learning of my father; and having seen many afflictions in the course of my days, nevertheless, having been highly favored of the Lord in all my days; yea, having had a great knowledge of the goodness and the mysteries of God, therefore I make a record of my proceedings in my days" (1 Nephi 1:1).

The family narrative is the "secret sauce" that holds families together. In those stories, we learn who we are and what we can become.

---

8 Marshall Duke, "The Stories That Bind Us: What Are the Twenty Questions?" *The Huffington Post*, http://www.huffingtonpost.com/marshall-p-duke/the-stories-that-bind-us-_b_2918975.html.

Chapter 10

OUCH! I FORGOT TO WRITE IT DOWN

KIM, A YOUNG MOTHER OF four, knows how important it is to keep records of her children's lives. She makes a baby book for each child and blogs about the adorable, profound, and funny things they say and do. One such event happened that she knew she should save for posterity. But life was crazy at the moment, so she scribbled the word *ouch* on a sticky note and went on attending to the craziness. A couple weeks later, she found the sticky note and could not remember what *ouch* referred to. That's how life goes. If you don't write it soon, the precious moment is gone forever.

In the early days of the Church, it was similarly difficult to write about experiences in the moment. If there was a mob charging the door or crickets chomping on crops, keeping a record may not have seemed like a priority. Such turbulent times of necessity meant writing about it later, and later is so much better than not all, because the only information we have about the past is what was written. Thus, in a very real sense, those who record history make history.

Wilford Woodruff was the premier record keeper in a time when "valuable records were lost due to unsettled conditions, when caretakers of the Church history apostatized and took records with them, and when faithful participants in the unfolding drama of the kingdom often kept no record at all. All this contributed to President Woodruff's great anxiety to keep a careful record of his own. For him, record-keeping was more than a casual activity; it was a religious service. He not only kept a diary and collected family records but also carried on an extensive correspondence."9

---

9 Dean C. Jesse, "Wilford Woodruff: A Man of Record," *Ensign*, July 1993.

In 1879 when Elder Woodruff lived in a remote area of Arizona, 165 miles from the nearest post office, he returned home after a short trip to find forty-one letters waiting for him. Because the post office was so far away, he persuaded the mailman to wait while he answered the letters. In a letter-writing marathon, Elder Woodruff wrote almost continuously for three days and nights and answered thirty-six of the letters. He said he wrote "until my hand and arm became numb and brain ceased to act."[10] Wilford Woodruff, responding to intuition and inspiration, knew: he who records history makes history. He also knew that if *he* didn't, there was no guarantee anyone else would. Record-keeping is an act of service to generations yet unborn.

Thomas Bullock kept the official record for the first group of pioneers who traveled to the Salt Lake Valley with Brigham Young in 1847. Brother Bullock made organized lists of who did what and when, adding many other details. If he hadn't kept a journal, these important facts would have been lost forever. In his journal, Luke Johnson, the Vanguard Company doctor, recorded his recipes for medicines as well as symptoms that indicated specific diseases. Appleton Harmon's journal included drawings of land formations he saw along the trail. He wrote of trials, testimony, and included copies of letters and blessings he received. Eliza R. Snow, the first secretary of the Relief Society, kept minutes in a bound book, providing facts about the beginnings of the Relief Society and much more. She also kept a personal journal, where she penned the words to ten hymns and other poems. The Lord commanded, "It shall be appointed unto him to keep the church record and history continually" (D&C 47:3). "Continually" means as it is happening.

Keeping records is never convenient. It takes work and time. The best accounts of events are recorded as close to the event as possible, which means that waiting until the dust settles puts history at risk. The time between the event and when it is recorded is critical because memories fade and details blur.

We give our thanks to our ancestors who kept written records. We don't judge what they wrote or their style or skill level. Even the great prophet Moroni worried about this. "Lord, the Gentiles will mock at these things, because of our weakness in writing" (Ether 12:23). Don't let it be so. Every written word is valuable and transmits perspective and culture—a written portrait of how life was way back then. Your personal

---

10 Ibid.

history freezes in time your speech patterns, your daily life, your hopes, dreams, desires, disappointments, adversities, and faith.

King Benjamin said, "I would that ye should remember that were it not for these . . . records . . . we must have suffered in ignorance . . . not knowing the mysteries of God. For it were not possible that our father, Lehi, could have remembered all these things, to have taught them to his children. . . . Were it not for these things, which have been kept and preserved by the hand of God . . . our fathers would have dwindled in unbelief" (Mosiah 1:3–5).

Since society often repeats the mistakes of the past, knowing history can help us avoid those mistakes. The personal purpose of keeping your own history is to extend your influence to next generations and to help you see your life in perspective. No matter your situation, no one is exempt from this duty. Present and future generations will thank you, and you'll thank yourself when you write more than just *ouch* on a sticky note.

Chapter 11

SELF-ESTEEM GONE WRONG

WHEN THE SELF-ESTEEM MOVEMENT WAS in vogue, many accepted it as truth. Mothers thought if they built each child's self-esteem by praising every action, making life full of fun and adventure, and being positive about everything the child did or said, then the children would reciprocate. Round and round they'd go, mother and child, building each other's self-esteem with mutual benefit and harmony.

This false philosophy of self-esteem also infiltrated the schools. "For decades, the prevailing wisdom in education was that high self-esteem would lead to high achievement. The theory led to an avalanche of daily affirmations, awards ceremonies and attendance certificates—but few, if any, academic gains."[11] Today society is reaping the effects of children who were praised when they didn't deserve it and were never told no. Now as adults, they feel entitled to everything they want without paying the price to earn it. It's been called the "gimme generation." In October 2011, writer Bill Whittle commented on the Occupy Wall Street protesters who were acting like "cry babies," not wanting to pay back their student loans and complaining about the success of large corporations. He attributed their actions to the self-esteem environment in which they were raised. Said he, "What we are seeing now is the self-esteem movement's chickens coming home to roost."[12]

The opposite of the self-esteem theory is the gospel-centered principle of individual worth, which is built on the foundation that

---

11 Michael Alison Chandler, "Education," *Washington Post*, http://articles.washington post.com/2012-01-15/local/35440671_praise-esteem-academic-standards.

12 Steve McGough, "OWS: The Self-Esteem Movement's Chickens Come Home to Roost," Radio Vice Online RSS, http://radioviceonline.com/bill-whittle-afterburner-video-occupy-wall-street-ows-three-days.

happiness comes in two ways: by loving God enough to do His will and by helping others become their best selves. Sound familiar? The Savior said, "Thou shalt love the Lord thy God with all thy heart, and with all thy soul, and with all thy mind. This is the first and great commandment. And the second is like unto it, Thou shalt love thy neighbour as thyself" (Matthew 22:37–39).

How a child is reared—to feel entitled or to understand the purpose in life—is determined by the adults in the child's environment. The difference in the two ways is that one is a theory and one is truth. The truth is, if you don't do good, you won't feel good about yourself no matter how you spin it.

Individual worth includes the ability to self-credit, to acknowledge to yourself that because of Heavenly Father's love and direction, you did something good or right. Individual worth means acknowledging when you do something wrong. Individual worth is knowing it's important to take responsibility, make restitution, and repent when you make an error or commit a sin. You say, "I'm sorry" and make your actions match your words. "Sorry is as sorry does."

Individual worth grows when you think of others' needs. Feelings of individual worth come when you treat others with respect. Why? Because, as you know, when you do good, you feel good.

Individual worth is an outgrowth of self-discipline, and self-discipline is a result of individual worth. Individual worth is courage and determination to achieve despite obstacles and opposition. Individual worth defines a person with character as one who keeps trying.

Individual worth is not placing false value on yourself. It is not arrogant, egotistical, snobbish, boastful, or competitive. Individual worth doesn't need to be stoked or stroked. Individual worth doesn't take, expecting others to give. Individual worth gives without needing to receive. Individual worth doesn't need to keep score, take credit, or place false value on things. Individual worth knows it's more important to *be* good than to *look* good. Individual worth nurtures self and others.

Discussing ways to nurture yourself comes with a caution. Self-nurturing has a counterfeit called self-indulgence. Self-indulgence puts more emphasis on *looking* good rather than on doing or being good. Self-indulgence doesn't help the Little Red Hen plant the wheat, pull the weeds, harvest, carry the wheat to the mill, or knead the flour into bread, but it expects to eat the just-out-of-the-oven bread, again describing the sense of entitlement of the gimme generation.

This defines our leisure-seeking, pleasure-seeking, thrill-seeking society in which one more possession, one more vacation, one more piercing or tattoo, or one more of whatever will make you feel good about yourself. And it doesn't matter how much stuff you have as long as you have more of it than someone else.

Self-indulgence is an empty vessel that can never be filled. You can never get enough of what you don't need. Self-gratification and ingratitude violate the laws of God. Individual worth, on the other hand, blooms when entering into and keeping covenants and commandments. Individual worth comes in being thankful and humble. Individual worth comes with faith that Heavenly Father exists, with understanding His attributes, and with seeking ratification that your course in life is pleasing to Him. Individual worth is realizing that everything you have, are, and can become comes from God.

Knowing you are a child of God gives you feelings of individual worth because you know His divine nature is in your spirit's DNA. You know He delights to bless those who love Him. "Hearken and hear, O ye my people, saith the Lord and your God, ye whom I delight to bless with the greatest of all blessings, ye that hear me" (D&C 41:1).

When you give credit to God and strive to live according to his purpose and plan, it is not your *self* you esteem but your Father in Heaven.

Chapter 12

ARE YOU WILLING?

You know how it works. There's been a death in the ward or neighborhood, and a clipboard is passed around in Relief Society asking for volunteers to help with the luncheon for the family after the funeral. Another week, a clipboard is passed around asking for volunteers to say the opening and closing prayers in Relief Society. Perhaps on the same clipboard is a list of service opportunities—to read to students at a nearby elementary school, to clean the ward or temple, to take a meal to a family who has just had a baby, to feed dinner to the full-time missionaries, to volunteer to substitute in Primary. That's why Relief Society is called *Relief* Society. It's an organization based on compassion that gives women opportunities to serve each other, the Church, and the community. And the best part is there's no pressure to sign up for anything. It's all voluntary.

On the day Joseph Smith organized the Relief Society, Emma Smith, Joseph's wife, was elected president. In her enthusiasm, and no doubt under the influence of the Holy Ghost, she exclaimed: "We are going to do something extraordinary." When asked what the extraordinary things would be, she gave as an example: "When a boat is struck on the rapids with a multitude of 'Mormons' on board, we shall consider that a loud call for relief; we expect extraordinary occasions and pressing calls."[13] That's what we are still about today, 172 years later; we consider these Relief Society clipboards a "loud call" for service and "expect extraordinary occasions and pressing calls." It's all about being *willing*.

Recently, Betty signed a clipboard list in Relief Society to take a meal to a family. She didn't know the family because she had just moved into

---

13 Janet Peterson and LaRene Gaunt, *Faith, Hope, and Charity*, American Fork, Utah: Covenant Communications, Inc., 2008, 5.

the ward. Whether she knew the family or not was of no consequence. She was following Emma Smith's example of being willing to serve people she'd never met when their "boat was struck on the rapids." The night before Betty was to take the dinner, the compassionate service leader called to say the family was doing much better and didn't need the meal. Knowing the people you serve is not necessarily important, being willing to serve *is*, whether you actually do it or not. Many Relief Society sisters who didn't sign any of the clipboards this time are still willing. (Signing clipboards has a lot to do with seasons and cycles of life and is unrelated to willingness.)

My sister and brother-in-law, Eileen and Wayne Moore, have served three full-time missions for the Church to inner-city San Francisco, inner-city Philadelphia, and Uganda, East Africa. After a year of being back home in Utah, they decided to serve again. Eileen was hoping for an easier mission call. She secretly hoped to be called to either Hawaii or Nauvoo and hoped for a temple mission—which would be like icing on the cake. Well, the call came to serve a temple mission in Nigeria.

Wayne and Eileen took a collective deep breath. Nigeria was so far away, but at least it was a temple mission. They prepared to go. But as more information came, Eileen realized this could be the most difficult mission yet because of political unrest in Nigeria. They would have to stay either in the temple or in their little apartment within the temple compound for the entire eighteen months.

In willingness, they said their good-byes and left for the MTC. After a few days, they received a message to go to the president's office. As they nervously sat across from him, he told them he had just received a call from Salt Lake informing him that their mission call had been changed. They were still called as temple missionaries, but instead of Nigeria they would serve in Kona, Hawaii. All you have to be is willing.

The prophet Moses commanded the people, saying, "Whosoever is of a willing heart, let him bring . . . an offering of the Lord" (Exodus 35:5). Did Betty's offer to take the dinner count as willing service even though she didn't have to do it? Certainly! Does it matter if Wayne and Eileen serve in Nigeria or Hawaii or in their own neighborhood? Not at all! All you have to be is willing.

Heavenly Father *willingly* sent His Only Begotten Son to a corrupt and fallen world. This Most Beloved Son followed His Father's pattern of *willingness*. He said: "For I came down from heaven, not to do mine own will, but the will of him that sent me" (John 6:38). But unlike the examples above, for the Savior there was no last-minute change in assignment.

You follow Jesus Christ's pattern of being willing to do the Father's will each week as you partake of the sacrament. In your heart you say, "I am '*willing* to take upon [me] the name of thy Son, and always remember him and keep his commandments'" (D&C 20:77). Whether halfway around the world or daily in your own home, you and I can show our love to Heavenly Father by our willingness to do His will.

Chapter 13

THE HAPPY-FACE ADVANTAGE

GIACOMO RIZZOLATTI, AN ITALIAN NEUROSCIENTIST, was the first to identify mirror neurons in the brain. All primates have them, but humans have the most sophisticated system by far. The human brain contains about one hundred billion mirror neurons that communicate with each other in staggeringly complex ways in fractions of a nanosecond. Mirror neurons got their name because they give us the ability to mirror others' feelings and sense others' moods as if they were our own.

The word *empathy* defines this phenomenon, which science hadn't been able to explain until the day Dr. Rizzolatti wired a monkey's brain to light up when the monkey performed an action such as picking up a peanut. What shocked Dr. Rizzolatti was when the monkey saw a lab assistant pick up a peanut, the same neurons that had fired when the monkey picked up a peanut fired when the lab assistant picked one up.

This was break-through science. This was more than vicariously experiencing something happening to someone else. The monkey's brain responded the same way whether he performed the action or merely watched someone else do it. Mirror neurons give us the ability to "read" each other's intentions and predict what others are going to do. That's why we cry in sad movies and smile when someone smiles at us. This complex transfer occurs without conscious thought.

We are built to feel each others' humanness, to share and be open. We aren't wired to be enemies—not politically, religiously, racially, or culturally. We only become enemies when we suppress or override what our mirror neurons are sensing.[14]

---

14 See Giacomo Rizzolatti and Laila Craighero, "The Mirror-Neuron System," http://psych.colorado.edu/~kimlab/Rizzolatti.annurev.neuro.2004.pdf.

Professor Paul Ekman spent a year learning to control the almost two hundred muscles in his face. As he gazed into a mirror, he identified eighteen types of smiles. He also found the brain prefers happy faces and recognizes happy expressions quicker than negative ones. This is called the "happy-face advantage."[15]

Smiling makes your face more attractive; it is the simplest and cheapest makeover possible. Smiling makes you feel better about yourself; smiling verifies the words your mother said to you on a day you were feeling blue—"Put on a happy face and you'll feel better." Smiling lifts moods even if you only smile at yourself in the mirror; smiling improves health; smiling decreases stress.

Dr. Ekman and a colleague did an experiment and practiced making the facial expressions of anger and distress, sitting across from each other for weeks. Finally, one of them told the other he was feeling awful. The other said he wasn't feeling well himself. So they began monitoring their body's respirations, blood pressure, and heart rates. While they thought they were just practicing making faces, they were actually making themselves angry and distressed. Facial expressions actually change the nervous system. An angry face generates anger; a distressed face causes distress.

Dr. John Gottman, who has studied marriage for forty years, can predict divorce with 94 percent accuracy after watching a videotape of a couple discussing a hot topic in their relationship. As he viewed these discussions second by second, he found that if the facial expression of disdain (disgust or contempt) shows for even the fleetest second in either spouse's face, there is almost no hope for the marriage. Even when the couple joke and act like they are in love, their true feelings show on their faces in microseconds.[16]

Edgar Allan Poe showed an intuitive grasp of this principle when in "The Purloined Letter," he wrote, "When I wish to find out how good or how wicked anyone is, or what are his thoughts at the moment, I fashion the expression of my face, as accurately as possible, in accordance with the expression of his, and then wait to see what thought or sentiments arise in my own mind or heart, as if to match or correspond with the expression."

Improving your ability to read faces will help you have better day-to-day interactions with family, friends, coworkers, and strangers. However,

---

15 See Daniel Goleman, *Social Intelligence*, New York: Bantam Dell, 2006, 44–45.
16 See "Research FAQ," The Gottman Relationship Institute, http://www.gottman.com/49853/Research-FAQs.html.

as important as being able to read others' faces may be, it's not about others' facial expressions. It's about your face, the face you see in the mirror, the face others see millions of times more often than you do. Your face is the mirror to your soul.

Happiness comes as a by-product of happy expressions, and happy expressions come from doing good. Abraham Lincoln is credited with saying, "When I do good I feel good." Moroni said the ability to be happy in this life carries over into the next life. "And then cometh the judgment of the Holy One upon them; and then cometh the time that he that is filthy shall be filthy still; and he that is righteous shall be righteous still; he that is happy shall be happy still; and he that is unhappy shall be unhappy still" (Mormon 9:14). The happy-face advantage is real.

Chapter 14

HUDDLING EMPEROR PENGUINS

"ICE WORLDS," ONE OF THE episodes in the *Planet Earth* series, shows life in an emperor penguin colony. (You can watch a two-minute video clip of the scene at http://www.bbc.co.uk/programmes/p0036tyc.)

After the mother lays the egg, the father comes and stands face-to-face, toe-to-toe in front of her. The mother gives the egg, which is resting on her feet, the slightest of nudges, and the father coaxes the egg up onto his feet. Then his big furry belly gently comes down over the egg, where it will incubate for four months. But every waddling step he takes brings risk to his unborn chick. If the egg rolls out, it will freeze in seconds.

If you visited an emperor penguin colony in Antarctica, you would see a landscape of whiteness with frozen snow and wind-carved ice, similar in effect to the red rock formations of Southern Utah. With that scene as a backdrop, imagine watching the exhausted and famished mother penguin successfully transfer the egg to the father. Then, in your mind, watch her return to the ocean. See the sun set, and feel darkness reign over Antarctica. Now you would observe a strange transformation as the penguin fathers shuffle into a huddle to generate enough heat to survive one-hundred-mile-an-hour winds and temperatures of seventy-five below zero. Nowhere on earth stays colder or darker for longer. Like a gigantic football team, they form tighter and tighter circles, perhaps ten penguins in a square yard, producing heat, bracing for winter blizzards. The penguins on the outside edge bear the full force of the storms and protect those in the safer, warmer middle.

The video shows the penguins huddling together in what looks like hump after hump of snow-covered black furry mounds in concentric circles. Their senses tell them their personal survival depends on their fellow penguins. Their instincts tell them that the next generation needs them to endure not eating, losing about one-third of their body weight, and doing nothing but standing with heads bowed in the tightest living conditions imaginable. That a penguin, let alone an egg, can survive these conditions defies probability.

After four months, spring comes to Antarctica. The eggs hatch, and miracle of miracles, each father, having eaten nothing for four months, has saved one meal in his stomach for his chick's first meal. He regurgitates it into his throat, and the chick reaches its beak up into the father's and is nourished. Then the mothers return from the sea—which is one hundred miles away—with their bellies full of fish. Then the fathers go to the ocean to feed, returning with their bellies full of fish. The babies now switch between parents' protective warmth. One parent stays while the other makes the long trek to the ocean for more fish. (It's kind of like one parent staying home with the baby while the other parent goes to the grocery store.)

These well-defined parenting roles nourish the next generation. How these penguins survive their hostile world can teach us how we can survive ours.

Every April and October we *huddle*—or, in the Lord's language, *gather*—in our homes, in meetinghouses, or in the Conference Center to watch general conference. Every six months we receive nourishment to withstand freezing worldly temperatures and family-threatening gale-force winds.

Without the guidance of general conference, it would be easy to get lost in a blinding blizzard, become disoriented, or let an egg slip away undetected. So we gather at the feet of Apostles and prophets for protection and also to hear counsel on how to nurture the next generation. We learn that parents are the first line of defense, working together, complementing each other's roles, taking turns incubating, feeding, shielding, and teaching by precept and example, so that the next generation will also be able to withstand the "consequence of evils and designs which do and will exist in the hearts of conspiring men in the last days" (D&C 89:4).

As we gather and enjoy each other's warmth of spirit, we may forget that our spiritual renewal and refreshment comes at a price others are paying. On the outside of the huddle, there are the fifteen latter-day Apostles, bearing the full force of the freezing winds and subzero temperatures, watching for those who stray, and keeping us united.

Words of counsel and revelation from general conference can help you survive your coldest and darkest trials. Though at times you will be exhausted and famished, gather with the Saints, add your warmth, and receive the cohesive protection provided.

Chapter 15

DID YOU HEAR GENERAL CONFERENCE?

AT LEAST EIGHT TIMES IN the New Testament, Jesus Christ teaches a doctrine and then invites his listeners to *hear*, not just listen to, His words. On one of those occasions, He said, "A sower went forth to sow. . . . Some seeds fell by the way side, and the fowls came and devoured them up. . . . [Others] because they had no root, they withered away. But other fell into good ground, and brought forth fruit, some an hundredfold, some sixtyfold, some thirtyfold. Who hath ears to hear, let him *hear*" (Matthew 13:4–9, Mark 4:14–20, emphasis added).

Jesus Christ is the Sower. He has sown His word through all dispensations of time through His prophets. He said, "What I the Lord have spoken, I have spoken, and I excuse not myself; and though the heavens and the earth pass away, my word shall not pass away, but shall all be fulfilled, whether by mine own voice or by the voice of my servants, it is the same" (D&C 1:38). General conferences of the Church are times to *hear* the word of the Lord through spoken word and music.

In conference we sing hymns of the Restoration—"We Thank Thee, O God, for a Prophet," "How Firm a Foundation," "Praise to the Man," "Now Let Us Rejoice," "Redeemer of Israel," "High on the Mountain Top." Singing with twenty-one thousand in the Conference Center thrills those who are privileged to be in attendance. Special numbers by the Tabernacle Choir and organists elevate and bring added portions of the Spirit. And members of the Church are not alone in their adulation of "America's Choir," as President Ronald Reagan named it, as is evidenced in the following conversation.

An usher for a Tabernacle Choir rehearsal noticed an Amish couple in their late twenties lined up with other tourists to hear the Thursday night rehearsal. The Amish couple caught the attention of the usher not only because of the woman's organdy bonnet but because the couple was holding hands, seeming very much in love. The usher started up a conversation:

Usher: Hello. Do you mind if I ask where are you from?

Amish man: Western Pennsylvania.

Usher: How long will you be in Salt Lake?

Amish woman: We will be here for a week.

Usher: You look very much in love.

Amish man (blushing slightly): We are on our honeymoon.

Usher: You are on your honeymoon and you chose to come to Salt Lake City?

Amish woman (with emotion): Yes. We feel so blessed to be here. The Mormon Tabernacle Choir is our favorite group!

The choir does stir emotion, as does the spoken word. You may have talks you can still hear in your mind—President Ezra Taft Benson's tremulous voice challenging the Church to flood the earth with the Book of Mormon; President Howard W. Hunter's almost-whispering voice imploring all members to have a current temple recommend no matter how far they live from the nearest temple; President Gordon B. Hinckley announcing small temples, the rebuilding of the Nauvoo Temple, or plans for building the Conference Center.

Many remember President Thomas S. Monson's clarion voice giving the follow-up account of Arthur, the young soldier who was killed in World War II, and of Arthur's mother, Mrs. Patten, or his direct and unmistakable call to the men of the priesthood to repent of anger. Will anyone ever forget President Monson's announcement of the change in age for young men to eighteen and young women to nineteen for full-time missionary service? How could anyone ever forget Elder Jeffrey R. Holland's passionate plea while holding in his hand the very Book of Mormon that Hyrum Smith read from in Carthage Jail just hours before he and his Prophet-brother were martyred? Can you hear in your mind Elder David A. Bednar in his first conference address teaching the Church about tender mercies or, depending on your age, Elders Bruce R. McConkie, David B. Haight, and Neal A. Maxwell giving their last conference testimonies?

You know there are special keys and responsibilities given to the presiding officers of the Church. How blessed we are to have living prophets who communicate the will of a living Father in Heaven. The words of the living prophet keep us current with God's will. The revelations given to Adam were not sufficient for Noah when he needed to build the ark. The revelations given to Noah were not sufficient to get Moses and the children of Israel through the wilderness. The revelations given to Moses were not sufficient to change the missionary age in 2012.

Do prophets' words come to you and fall by the wayside? A living prophet is of no value if we do not heed his counsel, and we have fifteen men we sustain as prophets, seers, and revelators. Because of technology, their words can be watched, listened to, and read over and over again, providing much opportunity to hear, contemplate, savor, and be nourished by the word with gladness.

Some listeners approach general conference as an all-you-can-eat buffet, picking and choosing what to *hear* and what to let fall by the wayside. We need deep roots of testimony so the prophets' words—all of them—fall on fertile soil because a prophet conveys the word of the Lord whether his name is Noah, Peter, Paul, Mormon, Moroni, Brigham Young, or any of the fifteen men seated on the front row of the Conference Center.

May each of us humbly acknowledge we have ears to *hear* the Sower's words and say in our hearts, "Speak, Lord; for thy servant *heareth*" (1 Samuel 3:9, emphasis added).

Chapter 16

WAYS TO ROB GOD

(PHRASES IN QUOTATION MARKS ARE direct quotes from scripture with perhaps a few pronouns changes.)

Heavenly Father: "Will a man rob God?"

Us: We hope not. Who would rob Thee?

Heavenly Father: "Yet you have robbed me."

Us: How? "Wherein have we robbed thee?"

Heavenly Father: "In tithes and offerings" (Malachi 3:8).

Us: In tithes and offerings?

Heavenly Father: Yes. Whether "of the herd or of the flock, the tenth shall be holy unto the Lord" (Leviticus 27:32). "Bring all your tithes into the storehouse" (Malachi 3:10).

Us: What exactly is a tithe?

Heavenly Father: One-tenth of your income, as it was when "Abraham paid tithes of one-tenth part of all he possessed" (Alma 13:15).

Us: We do want to obey Thy commandments. But the economy is really bad right now, and our finances are very tight. As it is, we can hardly make the payments on the house and cars and save a little for the children's education and our retirement.

Heavenly Father: "Prove me now herewith" (Malachi 3:10).

Us: You mean put you to a test?

Heavenly Father: Yes. "All the earth is mine" (Exodus 19:5). "I made the world" (Moses 6:51). "I [have] given you all things" (Genesis 9:3).

Us: We do not want to rob Thee, but it will be quite a sacrifice.

Heavenly Father: Today "is a day of sacrifice, and a day for the tithing of my people" (D&C 64:23). See for yourself "if I will not open you the windows of heaven, and pour you out a blessing, that there shall not be room enough to receive it" (Malachi 3:10).

Us: You will bless us with so much that we will not have room to store it?

Heavenly Father: Yes, and "he that is tithed shall not be burned at [the Second] coming" (D&C 64:23).

Us: We will put Thee to the test and exercise our faith to pay tithing.

Heavenly Father: It takes faith, not just money, to pay tithing. But it seems you have forgotten about fast offerings.

Us: Isn't tithing enough? How much are fast offerings?

Heavenly Father: The equivalent of the two meals you fast is the minimum. When you have plenty, as much as you can.

Us: That seems fair, but it's more money.

Heavenly Father: And more blessings. By choosing to fast and giving your fast offering, you help provide for the hungry, homeless, downtrodden, disabled, discouraged. I promise "your health shall spring forth speedily: and [my] righteousness shall go before you; [my glory] shall be your" guide (Isaiah 58:8). "Before you call, I will answer; and while you are yet speaking, I will hear" (Isaiah 65:24).

Us: We desire these blessings. We will pay both our tithes and fast offerings.

Heavenly Father: You rob me in another way.

Us: Oh. Is more money needed?

Heavenly Father: No, not your money but your time. The laborers in my vineyard are few compared to the work that needs to be done. Please do not withhold your labor from me.

Us: How do we labor for Thee?

Heavenly Father: "By love serve one another" (Galatians 5:13) at home, in your wards and stakes, and in private.

Us: How will we know how and whom to serve?

Heavenly Father: Accept callings, and my Spirit will guide you. Also, you can "do many things of your own free will, and bring to pass much righteousness" (D&C 58:27). It is not necessary that I "command in all things" (D&C 58:26).

Us: Not that we need a blessing for serving; we know service is its own reward, but you have said that you "delight to honor those who serve [Thee] in righteousness and in truth unto the end" (D&C 76:5).

Heavenly Father: "I will bless all those who labor in my vineyard with a mighty blessing" (D&C 21:9). "Inasmuch as you have done it unto one of the least . . . you have done it unto me" (Matthew 5:40).

"Give, and it shall be given unto you; good measure, pressed down, and shaken together, and running over, shall men give into your bosom. For with the same measure that [you give,] it shall be measured to you again" (Luke 6:38).

Us: We will give tithes and fast offerings, and we will serve Thee by serving our families and fellowmen in love.

Heavenly Father: You yet rob me.

Us: Is it more money or time?

Heavenly Father: Neither. It's your heart. "For in nothing doth man offend me, or against none is my wrath kindled, save those who confess not my hand in all things" (D&C 59:21). "Thou shalt thank the Lord Thy God in all things" (D&C 59:7).

Us: We will thank Thee and acknowledge Thy hand in all things. We thank Thee for Thy great plan of happiness, for this earth and the beauties of Thy creations, for Thy Son, Jesus Christ, and His Atonement, for the comfort and promptings of the Holy Ghost, for prophets living and dead, especially for the Prophet Joseph Smith and the restored gospel of Jesus Christ in these latter days, for our families, for the sealing ordinance of the temple, for the organization of the Church, for the scriptures, for Thine answers to our prayers, for the abundance of Thy tender mercies. May it never be said that we robbed Thee in any way. We do not want to be slothful servants. We willingly thank Thee for all we have and are—our bodies, our minds, our opportunities, even the growth Thou dost provide through adversity. "O Lord our God, we will give thanks unto thee for ever" (Psalm 30:12).

Chapter 17

AGENCY—ALMOST NOTHING MATTERS MORE

THE WORD AGENCY MAY BRING to mind the Central Intelligence Agency, an insurance agent, or becoming a free agent in professional sports. Yet the most important definition is "the ability and privilege to choose"—to act for yourself.

Agency is your most precious possession. Your agency allows you to choose not only right or wrong but also what you do with your mind and body minute by minute, day by day.

The absolute fact about agency is that every choice comes with a consequence. If you pick up one end of a stick (choice), you are also choosing the other end of the stick (consequence). Good choices lead to happiness and freedom. Bad choices lead to misery and bondage.

Two women had just finished a day of shopping at Las Americas Premium Outlet, which is located near the Mexican border. They were chatting about the bargains they'd found when all the cars in all the lanes of the freeway slowed abruptly. The women assumed there had been an accident. Soon, however, they saw what looked like a small army of border patrol guards forming a barrier across the freeway and stopping every vehicle. Some people were standing on the side of the road while their cars were searched. Others were allowed to continue on their way.

As the women inched closer to the unfolding scene, they saw two American-looking men ordered out of their vehicle, handcuffed, and forced to lie on the ground. While this was happening, other officers with drug-sniffing dogs searched the car. The guards rummaged through the men's possessions, took the evidence they found, pushed the vehicle to the shoulder of the freeway, and put the handcuffed men into a patrol car. Moments before, the two men had been free to come and go at will. Now, in handcuffs, they had lost a significant portion of their agency.

Agency is the God-given gift of choice. When you make good choices, your agency increases; you enjoy more rights, more options, more opportunities. When you make poor choices—such as smuggling drugs across an international border—you lose agency. Of course, it wasn't the border patrol guards who took away the drug-smugglers' agency; it was the smugglers themselves. The border patrol just enforced the consequences of the smugglers' unwise use of agency. The men thought they had been free, but in reality, being caught was just a matter of time.

Cause-and-effect is a true law of God and man. You choose your actions but can't choose what happens next. Even if you think no one will ever find out, someone knows. When you break a law or commandment, you live with guilt, fear, and anxiety that your secret deed will be discovered. That's not freedom. Committing an immoral or illegal act is voluntarily giving up portions of your agency, even if you haven't been caught yet. People who use their agency to break the laws of man and God build their own inner prisons, their own slave quarters.

Slavery was part of what caused the most costly war in United States history. (Civil wars are always the most devastating because all the casualties are from the same country.) Every aspect of slavery is wrong and evil, but one of the most despicable facts is that Africans sold other Africans into slavery. Initially, European traders captured Africans, but soon African rulers saw an opportunity and began to capture and sell fellow countrymen to the slave traders.

Ottobah Cugoano, who was about thirteen years old when he was kidnapped in 1770, had no doubt about the shared responsibility of Africans in the horrid slave business. Years later, after regaining his freedom, he wrote, "I must own, to the shame of my own countrymen, that I was first kidnapped and betrayed by some of my own complexion, who were the first cause of my exile and slavery."[17]

In the Civil War, deaths in the Union army were about 360,000. On the Confederate side, there were about 258,000. That brings the total of American soldiers lost, as countrymen inflicted death upon each other, to 618,000. We look with horror on such statistics and ask, "How could a nation do this to itself?

---

17 Tunde Obadina, "Slave Trade as Root to African Crisis," *Africa Economic Analysis*, www.afbis.com/analysis/slave.htm.

Like the Africans who sold other Africans into slavery, drug smugglers are willing to sell their fellow Americans—men, women, teens, perhaps even children—into the slavery of addiction. Addiction is like a civil war inside the addicted person, inside the family, inside society. Estimates suggest 23,000,000 people in the United States are addicted to illegal drugs. We look with horror on such statistics and ask, "How could a nation do this to itself?

Divorce is civil war between husband and wife. Abortion is civil war between mother and baby. Abuse and anger are civil wars between perpetrator and victim. Drugs and alcohol cause civil war between users, their minds and bodies, and everyone who loves them. The metal chains of the slave trade are no more real than the mental chains of addiction. All sap agency.

Heavenly Father has given you agency. As Nephi said, you are "free to choose liberty and eternal life, through the great Mediator of all men, or to choose captivity and death, according to the captivity and power of the devil" (2 Nephi 2:27). Wise use of agency empowers, inspires, and brings happiness and success. Foolish use of agency brings conflict, disappointment, failure, sadness, guilt, shame, and regret. Value your agency as you do your life. Protect it with good choices, and good consequences will follow.

Chapter 18

SEEING ADDICTION FOR WHAT IT IS

As I DROVE HOME ONE evening at dusk, first one eagle then another swooped down in front of me. I quickly pulled over to the side of the road and grabbed my camera. For the next thirty minutes, I watched an incredible scene unfold as eagle after eagle came from the northwest, circled a tall pine tree a couple of times, and landed in the tree. Never had I seen or imagined such an opportunity. I lost track after I counted twenty-five. It was unbelievable. I thought of calling the local news station to tell them to come photograph the tree full of eagles. I wanted to share this once-in-a-lifetime experience with the world. Soon I realized it was too dark to get photos, so I drove home, where I excitedly told Richard what I'd seen.

He listened and responded in a kind but skeptical voice, "Are you sure they were eagles?"

"Positive," I answered. "Do you know any other bird that has a five- to six-foot wingspan?"

"Can't say that I do," he replied. "I'd like to see them. Do you think they'll be there again tomorrow night?"

"I don't know," I answered, "but I'd like to go back and take binoculars."

The following night we arrived at the spot about the same time I had been there the night before, and there was already one eagle in the tree. "Look!" I said excitedly. Then another came, and another, and another.

Richard saw for himself. "Wow," he said in such a way that I knew he was surprised. Not that he didn't believe me, but twenty-five eagles in one tree is quite the fish story.

"Do you think they are bald eagles?" I asked.

"I don't know," he said. "Hand me the binoculars."

After a minute, he handed the binoculars back to me. "See for yourself." As I focused in on the tree, I could see five big birds, one very clearly. I studied the head to see what color it was. I looked for a long while—the birds' heads weren't white or golden but red. Then I realized my eagles were really vultures. What I thought I was pursuing was eagles—the birds that soar on the wind and dive at speeds of up to seventy-five miles an hour, the birds that were chosen to be our national emblem on June 20, 1782, by the Continental Congress, the birds that symbolize freedom, majesty, and strength. In truth, I was pursuing birds that circle wounded animals, patiently waiting for them to die, and then eat their rotting flesh.

A similar scene plays out for addicts. A substance or behavior blinds them to the fact that what makes them feel like they are soaring with the eagles—alcohol, drugs, shopping, gambling, eating, sex, pornography— is in reality vulture-like. The vulture of addiction circles overhead, waiting for the addict to participate in the addictive behavior again and again and again. Addiction is so prevalent today that most every family has experienced the loss of a son or daughter, husband or wife, sibling, cousin, aunt, or uncle to a substance or behavior.

As horrible as this is, the worst loss, of course, is to the individual. If the addiction is allowed to continue, the addict will experience loss in every aspect of life—loss of health, loss of youth, loss of good looks, loss of peace of mind, loss of respectability, loss of love, loss of family, loss of job, loss of potential and opportunity, and loss of the Spirit—to name only a few.

The scriptures speak of lost things—lost coins, lost tribes, lost inheritances, lost sheep, lost souls. Jesus Christ said, "The Son of man is come to *seek* . . . that which was lost" (Luke 19:10, emphasis added). The scriptures also tell of things that are found: the shepherds found "the babe wrapped in swaddling clothes" (Luke 2:12); Noah found grace; Alma found peace; Abraham found favor in the Lord's sight; the prodigal son "came to himself" (Luke 15:17) and found his way back. Obviously, lost things are nothing compared to lost people.

Lost and found people in parables are spoken of as lambs and sheep. Lost lambs and lost sheep are lost because they don't follow the Shepherd. The Savior asked, "What man of you, having an hundred sheep, if he lose one of them, doth not leave the ninety and nine in the wilderness, and go after that which is lost, until he find it?" (Luke 15:4). The Good Shepherd seeks lambs and sheep that are lost while caring for those who are safe in the fold.

Many who are partaking of vulture-like substances or behaviors want to follow the Shepherd and return to the fold but do not know how. They may feel embarrassed or fear they will not be accepted, or the addiction has robbed them of their agency and they cannot stop their addictive behavior. When sheep stray, wandering farther and farther afield, they come into contact with other lost sheep and become friends because they have their "lostness" in common. Instead of following the Shepherd to the safety of the fold, they keep following others who are lost "into forbidden paths and [stay] lost" (1 Nephi 8:28).

If you are involved in any addictive behavior or substance, pray to find your way back. Counsel with others who are safe in the Shepherd's fold. If these two steps don't help, get into a recovery program. If you love someone who is lost in addiction, keep praying even if everyone else has given up. Encourage him or her to regularly attend a twelve-step program, and go with him or her if that will help. Pray to know your role in your loved one's recovery.

Dan's older brother had come home from his mission with gifts for everyone in the family. Dan's gift was an intricately carved silver ring. The ring was precious to him because it symbolized his older brother's love. One night when he was washing his hands, he saw the ring wasn't on his finger. Although it was late and he had to get up early, he searched his room from top to bottom without success. He prayed to find the ring. The next day at school, he searched his locker, and friends helped him search the soccer field where they had played the day the ring was lost. That night he prayed fervently again.

In the morning, he saw in his mind where to look—the black garbage bag he had filled while cleaning up the backyard where his dog lived. He knew if he wanted the ring, he had to look in the bag. He braced himself for an unpleasant task, opened the bag, held his breath, and used a stick to look through it. He'd take a deep breath, hold it, search with the stick, then close the bag, take another deep breath, and search some more. When he was almost overcome by the smell and ready to give up, he saw something glisten. He had no choice but to put his hand in the bag in order to pull out the shiny object. As he gratefully washed and washed and washed the ring, he marveled that it was found.

Heavenly Father always knows where His lost children are, so no one is ever truly "lost." In His abundant love, He has provided a way whereby addicts in even the dirtiest and smelliest environments can, through repentance and the Atonement, become clean. Jesus Christ "is come to seek and to save that which was lost" (Luke 19:10). If you are figuratively in a black garbage bag, if vultures are your friends, with the help of the Holy Ghost and prayer you can find yourself, be washed clean, and soar with eagles.

Chapter 19

THIS TIME, LET'S LEARN THE LESSON QUICKLY

BURY THE CHAINS IS A book about how the chains of slavery were buried in the British Empire. It all began in 1787 when twelve men met in a London print shop to organize themselves against slavery.

> If, early that year, you had stood on a London street corner and insisted that slavery was morally wrong and should be stopped, nine out of ten listeners would have laughed you off as a crackpot. The tenth might have agreed with you in principle but assured you that ending slavery was wildly impractical: the economy would collapse. . . .
>
> Within a few short years, however, the issue of slavery had moved to center stage in British political life. There was an abolition committee in every major city or town. . . . More than three hundred thousand Britons were refusing to eat slave-grown sugar. Parliament was flooded with far more signatures on abolition petitions than it had ever received on any other subject.[18]

In 1807, the British parliament outlawed the slave trade, and in 1838, they ruled slavery illegal.

The American Civil War began about fifty years after Britain's Parliament officially ended the slave trade and about twenty-three years after the British Empire outlawed slavery. The question is, why, when the morality of slavery had been settled in Great Britain, didn't the United States learn this lesson without having to fight a civil war?

There is a parallel today. Another form of slave trade and slavery is being practiced in both Great Britain and the United States. Again,

---

18 Adam Hochschild, *Bury the Chains*, Houghton Mifflin Company, 2005, 7.

Great Britain has taken the lead in burying the chains. What chains? What form of slavery? It is pornography.

On July 22, 2013, Prime Minister David Cameron of Great Britain spoke passionately about how Internet pornography is corroding away childhood. He is proposing new laws with strict guidelines for Internet providers with the goal to make the Internet safer for children and families.

How long will it take Americans to follow? Where are we on the continuum? Are we at the stage of the twelve men in the London print shop? Are we willing to figuratively boycott sugar and sign petitions? Where is the American equivalent of Prime Minister Cameron who will stand up and say, "Enough is enough"?

On December 30, 2010, a Reuters news release reported that "China shut down more than 60,000 pornographic websites this year, netting almost 5,000 suspects . . . in its campaign against material deemed obscene." The article continued by saying that the "smutty and lewd content" presented a threat to the "emotional health of children. . . . Our campaign has been a great success, and this has not been achieved easily. . . . We have made the Internet environment much cleaner than before."[19]

Mark Kastelman, a researcher and expert in mind-body science, wrote, "Pornography is powerful because it takes advantage of and taps into intense emotional, biological, and chemical connections throughout the brain and the entire body. We are born with many of these connections 'pre-wired' or 'pre-set' to switch on at certain times in our development. Pornography seeks to twist the truth and 'mimic' or 'counterfeit' this built-in attraction. Its goal is to ignite, excite, and exploit these natural built-in urges and desires. . . . Internet porn is a drug, and pornographers are drug dealers."[20]

He asserts that pornography makes men stupid by narrowing the brain and robbing it of "logic, reason, and sound judgment (regardless of age)." He says that pornography is so powerful that "nothing else matters but satisfying the fiery urges the porn has ignited." He states that pornography can be so addicting that only one hour of Internet porn can hook another victim.[21]

---

19 "China Shuts over 60,000 Porn Websites This Year," Reuters, http://www.reuters.com/article/2010/12/30/china-internet-idUSTOE6BT01T20101230.

20 Mark Kastleman, "The 'Brain Science' Behind Internet Porn Addiction," Net Nanny, http://www.netnanny.com/learn_center/article/175/.

21 Ibid.

And victims there are aplenty. Pornography statistics testify of the hard-to-stomach reality[22]:

- American children begin consuming hardcore pornography at an average age of 11.
- Four out of five 16-year-olds regularly access pornography online.
- The pornography industry is a $97 billion business worldwide.
- The pornography industry is a $13 billion business in the United States.
- Internet pornography in the United States is a $3 billion industry.
- Every second $3,075.64 is being spent on pornography.
- Every second 28,258 Internet users are viewing pornography.
- "Every 39 minutes, a new pornographic video is made in the United States."[23]

While we wait for courageous political leaders in the United States who will follow Great Britain's and China's lead, you can lead out in your own sphere of influence:

Understand that addiction is a chronic disease of the brain that causes physical, psychological, social, intellectual, and spiritual dysfunction. It negatively affects memory and motivation. "Like other chronic diseases, addiction often involves cycles of relapse and remission."[24]

Acknowledge that anyone, including yourself, who seeks pornography is addicted. Addicts must seek help by attending a twelve-step program, receiving counseling, or joining a support group. Addicts can become clean by staying sober. (Sober isn't just about alcohol. Sober means a person is not using the addictive substance.)

Teach your children, just as you do with addictive substances that violate the Word of Wisdom, not to use pornography because it harms the body and mind.

Move all computers and televisions to public areas of your home. Password-protect access.

Check the history on your children's cell phones often and have a "docking" rule. Every night every cell phone is docked in the parents' bedroom at a precise time.

---

22 "Internet Safety 101," Enough Is Enough, http://www.internetsafety101.org/Pornographystatistics.htm.
23 Internet Filter Review, 2006.
24 "Definition of Addiction," ASAM, http://www.asam.org/for-the-public/definition-of-addiction.

Become involved in community groups who fight against incursions of pornography. Help move the issue of pornography center stage.

Petition local and national governments to protect the minds of men, women, teens, boys, and girls from all forms of pornography.

Support zero tolerance in the workplace.

Involve yourself and your children in family history and temple work to claim Elder David A. Bednar's promise of spiritual protection. He said by participating in this great redeeming work, the living can also be redeemed and saved.

Read Elder Bednar's talk "The Hearts of the Children Shall Turn" as a family. Pay special attention to his words *invite*, *encourage*, *urge*, and *promise*.[25]

---

25 See http://www.lds.org/ensign/2011/11/the-hearts-of-the-children-shall-turn.

Chapter 20

YOUR RIGHT TO VOTE

IN THE UNITED STATES TODAY, between 1 and 60 percent of Americans choose to use their right to vote, depending on whether it is a primary or general election, county, state, or national.

At Colonial Williamsburg, Virginia, two actors portraying Thomas Jefferson and Patrick Henry provided their audience with a live debate and a powerful lesson on the privilege of voting.

Patrick Henry spoke first and explained that in the 1780s, Virginia law required that every citizen attend church service at least once a month. The purpose of the law "was not only to reinforce . . . the gospel of Jesus, it was also to ensure that we had a better informed citizenry." Church services included a time for news of when official announcements and bills before the legislature would be discussed. "By regularly attending church, everyone would be able to hear this news, whether they were able to read newspapers or no," said Mr. Henry.[26]

As the debate proceeded, the audience learned that both Henry and Jefferson had introduced bills in the Virginia General Assembly on the subject of a religious tax to pay ministers and maintain church buildings. "Perhaps most importantly of all," said Mr. Henry, "those tax monies were applied to the care of the poor and the needy within society—the widows, the orphans, the sick, the dying, and the indigent—ever the domain of religion and not of government."[27]

Mr. Henry's plan stated, "All heads of household will . . . pay an annual, very moderate, reasonable assessment [tax] towards religion. However, they will be able to choose to which church . . . they wish those

---

26 "Patrick Henry on Religion," Colonial Williamsburg, http://www.history.org/media/podcasts_transcripts/PatrickHenryonReligion.cfm.
27 Ibid.

monies to be applied. Thus, I believe that *all* denominations will flourish around the countryside."[28] However, the choice of which church citizens could assign their tax money to was limited to four mainstream Protestant churches—Methodist, Baptist, Congregational, or Presbyterian.

After listening to Patrick Henry for a long time, Thomas Jefferson interrupted. "Mr. Henry, we have more in common than you might think. I do not deny the virtue, the morals of Christian principles, and yet it is not the duty of our government, it is not the duty of any bill of rights to assert that one particular religious opinion should be held over any others. Mr. Henry, we should not assume that as the [head of the] family of man He is to recognize one particular religious opinion over another. He is the God of all."

Mr. Jefferson desired that Catholics, Jews, and other religions should also receive tax monies for their support and to aid their poor. He said, "Let us recognize that *every* individual has the right to pursue their religious opinion as they choose and that *no* tax . . . should be drawn from the people to support one particular church, or . . . religious opinion over another."

After Mr. Jefferson had eloquently made these points, Mr. Henry nodded with a polite bow to Mr. Jefferson and asked if he would be willing to have the people in the theater vote to express the plan with which they most agreed. Mr. Jefferson politely bowed and answered with a smile, that yes, indeed, he would find such a vote to his liking. By the feeling of excitement in the theater, it was apparent that the approximately two hundred men, women, and children in attendance wanted to express their opinions by voting.

"Very well," said Mr. Henry. "Will all the men, please stand." A gasp of shock swept over the audience as the women remembered that in 1780 they did not have the right to vote.

Then Mr. Henry said, "Will all the boys and young men under age twenty-one please be seated."

Next Mr. Henry said, "Slaves, Indians, and persons of color, please be seated." The audience again expressed amazement, realizing in 1780 only "whites" could vote.

Then Mr. Henry said, "Gentlemen, if you are not Methodist, Baptist, Congregationalist, or Presbyterian, please be seated." About half of the men sat down.

---

28 Ibid.

Mr. Henry then instructed the men left standing that to vote they had to own property—either eighty acres of unimproved ground, forty acres of improved property with at least one building on it, or own a home as his primary residence in town. Three men remained standing.

At that, Thomas Jefferson stepped forward and said to the three men, "And gentlemen, there can be no mortgage on the property." Two of the three sat down. Out of a theater full of potential voters, only one man could vote!

The Fourteenth Amendment to the Constitution freed the slaves in 1868. The Nineteenth Amendment gave women the right to vote in 1920. Today men and women age twenty-one and older of all races, religions, and social status can vote, which is just one of many precious freedoms we enjoy as citizens of the United States of America. Voting each election day is a liberty to be valued.[29]

---

29 See also "Thomas Jefferson vs. Patrick Henry," Colonial Williamsburg, http://www.history.org/media/podcasts_transcripts/JeffersonvsHenry.cfm.

Chapter 21

THE OPPOSITE EXTREMES OF KINDNESS

"WHAT DO YOU THINK IS the most important ingredient in a good marriage? Many people would probably say . . . communication. . . .[But] today many scholars say that the most important element in a successful marriage is kindness. Kindness includes looking for the good in all the ordinary dealings with a partner."[30]

Kindness is the most important attribute in all relationships—parent to child, child to parent, sibling to sibling, friend to friend, boss to employee, employee to boss, neighbor to neighbor.

Bob and Sheri Stritof, who write for About.com, know something about marriage and divorce. They got married, they divorced, and they remarried each other. They assert, "Without kindness in your relationship, your marriage won't last."[31] The same is true of any relationship—without kindness it probably won't last, and if it does last, the relationship will not be happy or healthy. A good rule of life is to treat others with kindness, not because they are kind to you but because you are a kind person, and that's what kind people do. Kindness builds strong relationships and benefits the kind person.

Allen Luks, executive director of Big Brothers/Big Sisters of New York City and author of *The Healing Power of Doing Good*, studied responses from 3,296 volunteers who were asked seventeen questions about how they felt when they did a kind act. Luks concluded, "Helping contributes to the maintenance of good health, and it can diminish the

---

30 "Family Life, The Marriage Garden, Kindness Builds Strong Marriages," University of Arkansas Division of Agriculture, http://www.arfamilies.org/family_life/marriage/kindness_strong_marriages.htm.

31 "Sheri and Bob Stritof," About.com, http://marriage.about.com/bio/Sheri-Bob-Stritof-275.htm.

effect of diseases and disorders both serious and minor, psychological and physical."[32]

He further explained that 90 percent of respondents told of euphoric feelings followed by a feeling of calmness that came after doing a kind act. Luks called this feeling a "helper's high" because endorphins, the body's natural painkillers, are released and cause a feeling of well-being, which reduces stress. Someone said, "Kindness, like a boomerang, always returns." Kindness is also contagious. You've heard of starting a kindness chain and of doing random acts of kindness.

Primary children sing "Kindness Begins with Me." Everyone can be kinder and knows how to be kinder. When we aren't as kind as we know we could be, it is usually because we prioritize our own needs, wants, and feelings over another's.

We all know the basics of kindness. If someone asks you for help, kindness means responding quickly to his or her need. Kindness serves.

Kindness shares. "Freely ye have received, freely give" (Matthew 10:8).

If someone is speaking to you, kindness means focusing on that person with your eyes, ears, brain, and heart. Kindness listens.

Kindness means accommodating others' wants, not giving what you would want but rather what the person wants. Kindness acknowledges individuality.

A few years ago, a friend who was moving across the country gave us two white nightstands, a white dresser, and two matching white and silver lamps. I was thrilled and thought a white wooden bed would make the bedroom look beautiful. I soon found, however, that I could not match the wood. So I started looking for a white metal bed. I went to many stores, but no one had what I pictured in my mind—a classy-looking, slightly ornate, white, durable (I want to say *heavy)* metal bed. Furniture salespersons in store after store tried to get me to buy a bed they had, but that was not what I wanted.

Then I went to a store I'd never been in before. A woman approached with a smile and asked how she could help. I explained what I wanted. She said, "I think I can find a bed just like what you have described," and showed me some photos in catalogs. She didn't try to up-sell me or down-sell me. She wanted me to have what I wanted. I felt validated. Every time I'm in that bedroom, I remember her kindness in helping

---

32 "The Healing Power of Doing Good: The Health and Spiritual Benefits of Helping Others," December 2004, http://melbabenson.com/articles.php.

me get what I wanted. She had respect for my wants. (And interestingly enough, six or seven years later, a new woman moved into our ward. I knew I had seen her before and felt immediate warmth toward her. As I sat by her in Relief Society, I scoured my brain to remember how I knew her. A few minutes later, I whispered, "Did you ever work at a furniture store in Murray?")

We have a whiteboard in our kitchen, where I keep a list of items needed from the grocery store. Richard adds to the list—kind of as a joke—things he knows I won't buy because I'm always imposing "healthy" foods on him. When I purchase an item on the list, I erase it. And, in my defense, I do buy an item or two from his list now and then. But, basically, his wants stay on the list ad infinitum. For Christmas, our son and daughter-in-law bought him all the items on the list—Oreos, potato chips, malt, bacon, real mayonnaise "not fat-free or low-fat," and coconut-pineapple ice cream. Richard was ecstatic. He smiled, laughed, and talked about it for weeks! Thanks, Dan and Ellen.

Responding to needs is a definite expression of kindness, as is the spoken word. Kindness is shown in "thank you," "please," and "how may I help?" Kindness is also shown in words you don't say. Knowing when to keep silent is as important as knowing when to speak and what to say. Your mother always said, "If you can't say something kind, don't say anything at all." James wrote: "Speak not evil one of another" (James 4:11). The hymn says, "Let us oft speak kind words to each other" (*Hymns*, no. 232).

Kindness is *thinking* kindly as well as acting and speaking kindly. Kindness looks for the good in others and gives compliments. Kindness keeps confidences. Kindness rejoices with others in their happy times and mourns with them in their sad times. Kindness is patient in taking turns.

Jason, age thirteen, and his mother were in the baggage claim area of a large airport filling out a report because their luggage hadn't arrived. As Jason's mother was handing the form to the clerk, a man stomped in, pushed Jason aside, and began to swear at the clerk. Punctuated by expletives, he said, "You are the most incompetent airline in the world. I demand you find my luggage now. My limousine driver has been waiting ten minutes. I will not be delayed by your inefficiency." After the clerk had done as much as she could, the man marched out, telling everyone— as if they hadn't heard—how wrongly he had been treated. Jason looked at his mother and said, "Rich people think they can get away with being unkind." True kindness is colorblind, age-blind, social-status blind, economically blind, and educationally blind.

Nevertheless, sometimes kindness is not that simple. Kindness can be complicated and may require courageous actions that, on the surface, may seem unkind. The admonition to say only kind words may not always be true if it means never discussing problems or whitewashing serious issues. Please consider three illustrations.

Illustration 1: My sister Sheila and I have a close relationship. One day I asked her if she would trim my eyebrows because they were very bushy and my eyesight is not good enough to do it myself. She kindly agreed and did it right then. While she was trimming, she said, "I think you should get a ten-power magnifying mirror. You have some errant hairs here and there. Make sure you get a lighted one." That afternoon, I bought such a mirror, came home, plugged it in, and saw my magnified, frightful reflection in the mirror. Was she being kind by telling me the truth? Absolutely!

Illustration 2: After an author submits a book to a publishing company, the publishing company sends the manuscript to a number of reviewers who evaluate the potential of the manuscript and give suggestions. (The reviewer doesn't know the author's name, and the author doesn't know the reviewers' names.) This book you are reading went to three reviewers, and Covenant sent me copies of their reviews. One review was mostly complimentary, giving a few suggestions. One gave a few more suggestions. One gave many suggestions and was very critical of certain chapters, suggesting they be fixed or deleted. One of this reviewer's comments was "The chapter on being lost goes nowhere," which is heavy criticism and actually very funny. (When you read the chapter, you can decide if it now goes somewhere. I've changed the chapter title to "Seeing Addiction for What It Is.") If the goal of an author is to produce a book that will benefit readers, critical reviewers can help the author improve the manuscript. Even an outright rejection can encourage the author to rewrite and improve the manuscript. J. K. Rowling received twelve rejection letters before the first Harry Potter book was published, and it is reported that the *Chicken Soup for the Soul* authors received thirty-three rejections.

Illustration 3: The admonition that kindness speaks kindly may keep you from addressing problems that need to be addressed. The oft-used image of not talking about the elephant in the room allows the problem to go unresolved. When important but sensitive information needs to be communicated, talk about it. For example, if you have evidence that someone is struggling with drugs, pornography, or alcohol, it is unkind to do nothing. If you are "kind" at the expense of being helpful, you are not kind. Rather you are enabling the person to continue in a destructive pattern. When I was a young mother, a friend confided in me that she was thinking of ending her life and asked me not to tell anyone. I assumed she was getting help and that her family knew. I kept the confidence but attended her funeral.

Being kind means knowing and understanding that kindness includes being gracious and congenial and accommodating others' needs and wants with wisdom and prudence. Kindness encompasses life's most difficult problems, situations we hope we never have to face, that require courage and firmness to bring to another's attention. Kindness demands that if someone is on a collision course with addiction or depression, we need to be proactive in providing help. Responding appropriately in this wide spectrum of kindness is vital to healthy relationships.

Chapter 22

HOW STAINS AND SINS ARE REMOVED

DURING THE TESTIMONY MEETING THAT followed the blessing of a baby, a visitor and relative of the baby bore her testimony. She mentioned that some family members were more active in the Church than others and that divorces had caused hurt feelings, rifts, and challenged relationships. She expressed hope that rebuilding and repairing relationships among family members would start so the negativity of the past would not be passed on to the new generation. She expressed hope that "it would all come out in the wash." Perhaps she didn't realize the profound significance of this offhanded, colloquial cliché, but she spoke truth.

All misunderstandings, hurt feelings, slights, physical and emotional pains, loneliness, questionings, disappointments, even sins can ultimately come out in the wash.

Ruth was taking clean, dry clothes out of the dryer when she noticed marks on the four new shirts her husband had just worn for the first time and on other items, including a favorite tablecloth. It looked like someone had taken a pen and drawn lines on them in erratic patterns. In the bottom of the dryer, Ruth saw a pen.

She had to try to remove the stains. She tried several cleaning products in her cupboard and scrubbed. The lines stayed the same. She tried other concoctions with no luck. Next she sprayed every line, maybe fifty or so, with a spray product and let the clothes sit for several hours, but the lines remained the same. Then she filled the washer with hot water, put in a heavy-duty detergent, added a generous cupful of color-fast bleach, put the clothes back in the washer, watched them agitate for a few minutes, stopped the washer, and let them sit overnight.

The next morning she reached into the now cold water and pulled out the blue shirt, intending to scrub each and every pen line again. To her amazement, the lines were gone. The yellow, green, and gray shirts had only a few very light lines. The tablecloth looked bright and good as new.

We can become like them. That great laundering event—lovingly, graciously, and amazingly offered and completed—begins when eight-year-olds become accountable and are baptized for the remission of sins. This laundering begins as converts over age eight enter the waters of baptism. That's not all: those who come with repentant, humbled hearts can experience this laundering every week by worthily partaking of the sacrament.

As you know, the soaping, scrubbing, bleaching, soaking, and cleansing of the Atonement of Jesus Christ make it possible for us to become clean. With loving respect, we could refer to him as the Great Laundryman. It's scriptural. Malachi 3:2 reads, "But who may abide the day of his coming? and who shall stand when he appeareth? for he is like a refiner's fire, and like *fullers' soap*" (emphasis added). And Mark 9:3 follows up on the concept: "And his raiment became shining, exceeding white as snow; so *as no fuller on earth can white them*" (emphasis added).

Some marks didn't come out of the shirts, but the yellow shirt didn't worry about the green shirt or the gray shirt or the blue shirt. It's not our job to worry about the divine process of cleansing that is happening to family, friends, and neighbors. Our divine personal and private cleansing is between the Great Laundryman and each individual. Some of us may need to submit ourselves to more scrubbing and bleaching; some may not be cleansed in this life because they refuse to come unto the Laundryman.

In the most recent revelation in the Doctrine and Covenants, section 138, President Joseph F. Smith said, "I beheld that the faithful elders of this dispensation, when they depart from mortal life, continue their labors in the preaching of the gospel of repentance and redemption, through the sacrifice of the Only Begotten Son of God, among those who are in darkness and under the bondage of sin in the great world of the spirits of the dead. The dead who repent will be redeemed, through obedience to the ordinances of the house of God, and after they have paid the penalty of their transgressions, and are washed clean, shall receive a reward according to their works, for they are heirs of salvation" (D&C 138:57–59).

The pen marks—anger, ingratitude, withholding affection, dishonesty, unkindness, judgmental thoughts and actions, participating in unrighteous media, crimes, and the sins of the world—can be removed from our souls. We can become clean because of the marks in the Savior's hands.

Joseph Smith and Oliver Cowdery saw the resurrected Jesus Christ and heard Him speak of their sins. "His voice was as the sound of the rushing of great waters, even the voice of Jehovah, saying: I am the first and the last; I am he who liveth, I am he who was slain; I am your advocate with the Father. Behold, your sins are forgiven you; you are clean before me; therefore, lift up your heads and rejoice" (D&C 110:3–5).

However, just hoping "it will all come out in the wash" isn't enough. "You are clean before me" is the blessing of being forgiven and could be stated: "Your repentance has been accepted." Repentance is a painful process whereby we prove to our Father in Heaven, through changed behavior and increased faith and actions, our intense desire to be forgiven. As we repent, we have the privilege of coming under the umbrella of the Atonement to be washed clean without spot or stain. If you think it's too late, it is not. Even heat-sealed, indelible pen marks can be removed.

Chapter 23

YOUR LOVE LANGUAGE IS SPOKEN HERE

PRIMARY CHILDREN SING ABOUT A language everyone can speak in a song by Janice Kapp Perry, "Love Is Spoken Here." The title also tells where love is to be spoken—*here*. Wherever I am I should be speaking the language of love. There is also a play on the word *here* to give another meaning—love is spoken, hear. At times, it may seem your loving words aren't heard, and there's a reason for that. People hear, feel, accept, receive, and perceive love in very different ways.

Gary Chapman wrote *The Five Love Languages*[33] to explain the fundamental problems in receiving or perceiving love. His thesis is that "if you express love in a way your spouse [or sister or brother or friend or parent] doesn't understand, he or she won't realize you've expressed your love at all. The problem is that you're speaking two different languages. Perhaps your husband needs to hear encouraging words, but you feel cooking a nice dinner will cheer him up. When he still feels down, you're puzzled. Or, maybe your wife craves time with you—time away from the kids and television. The flowers you give her just don't communicate that you care."[34]

Understanding this principle led me to watch for ways in which Heavenly Father expresses love, since He is the originator of love and speaks everyone's love language. His "techniques," for want of a better word, gave me ideas about how to feel His love more abundantly and how to use His example to show greater love to others. Even though His ways are definitely not our ways, for comparison's sake, let's compare Dr. Chapman's five love languages—words of affirmation, quality time, receiving gifts, acts of service, and physical touch—to Heavenly Father's

---

33 Chicago: Northfield Publishing, 1995.
34 Ibid., back cover.

ways, hopefully to understand His love a little better. By doing so, perhaps we can communicate our love for others more effectively.

Divine Words of Affirmation

The way our Father in Heaven speaks provides a perfect example of how to compliment, validate, and show love using the spoken word. He said at the baptism of His Only Begotten: "Thou art my beloved Son, in whom I am well pleased" (Mark 1:11). He declared his kinship by using the word "Son" and showed his affection in the word "beloved." When He introduced His Son marking the beginning of this last dispensation, He said, "[Joseph,] this is My Beloved Son. Hear Him" (Joseph Smith-History 1:17). This time He added a third and fourth aspect of divine communication. The Father used the most identifying word any person has, a name—"Joseph"—and gave him instruction to "Hear Him," or "listen to my Son, who will instruct you," which gave Joseph permission to ask his question.

We can likewise bestow love through words of affirmation by using the person's name, by lovingly stating our relationship, by using exact adjectives and verbs to praise specific actions, by inviting dialogue, by giving helpful information, by teaching, by listening, and by responding to questions with sensitivity.

Divine Time

Heavenly Father is perfect in giving time as He has infinite, one-eternal-round time. Through His Spirit, He can spend one-on-one time to inspire, give direction, and show love to each of His children without limit. Time—past, present, future—is concurrent with Him. For finite mortals, giving time is harder because we're always pressed for more. We speak of time in two categories—quantity and quality. We should aim for quality time, yet that is most often impossible without quantity. You can't say, "I have five minutes. Tell me what's troubling you." Since money can't buy more minutes, giving time is one of the greatest evidences of love and is a love language that speaks to almost everyone. How can we emulate godlike giving of time? Perhaps by listening longer, being patient longer, waiting longer, being available more often, and being willing to spend all the time it takes.

Divine Gift-Giving and Receiving

It is relatively easy to identify people whose love language is receiving gifts because these people give well-thought-out gifts to others. To show your love to such people, watch for clues about things they like, then plan and prepare. Give them something meaningful not to you but to them. You can raise your gift-giving awareness by thinking about the quality of Heavenly Father's gifts and realizing the efforts to which He goes to bestow tender mercies. Some of Heavenly Father's gifts are providing a Savior so that we can repent, giving a member of the Godhead to be our constant companion, answering prayers, providing temples, covenants, commandments, scriptures, and ultimately eternal life. In fact, the greatest gift we can give anyone is the opportunity to learn the gospel and obtain knowledge of God our Eternal Father, His Son Jesus Christ, and the Holy Ghost.

Divine Physical Touch

Physical touch is one of Heavenly Father's best gifts. Nephi said, "I am encircled about eternally in the arms of his love" (2 Nephi 1:15), which sounds like a long, heavenly hug. The Holy Ghost gives us spiritual caresses, sometimes in physical ways. His tangible affection has been described as "a warm blanket around my shoulders," "a spiritual embrace," "a feeling that my heart is full to overflowing." The two disciples on the road to Emmaus said, "Did not our heart burn within us?" (Luke 24:32). Another very beautiful physical touch is the laying on of hands that accompanies receiving priesthood blessings and being set apart for callings. As we carefully and appropriately use the gift of touch—a hug, a kiss, an arm around the shoulder, the taking hold of a hand, or even a pat on the back—we validate others and convey the touch of the divine.

Divine Acts of Service

Heavenly Father gives acts of service in the macro and micro as is evidenced by galaxies and gnats. He serves with endless variety in landscapes, cloud formations, glorious and powerful elements interacting in time and space, flowers in endless shapes, colors, and fragrances, and magnificent creatures that fly, swim, and roam the earth. His greatest act of service is His plan for the salvation of every one of His children. It's a plan He calls "happiness" because He wants us to be happy. "Men are, that they might have joy" (2 Nephi 2:25). This happiness and ultimate joy come because "He gave his only begotten Son" (John 3:16) and His Son did not disappoint. As King Benjamin prophesied over a century before its fulfillment, "For behold, the time cometh, and is not far distant, that with power, the Lord Omnipotent who reigneth, who was, and is from all eternity to all eternity, shall come down from heaven among the children of men, and shall dwell in a tabernacle of clay, and shall go forth amongst men, working mighty miracles, such as healing the sick, raising the dead, causing the lame to walk, the blind to receive their sight, and the deaf to hear, and curing all manner of diseases" (Mosiah 3:5). Our finest act of service comes when we share this knowledge by letting the Light of Christ shine in our actions, serving others as He would—in their own love language.

Working in the temple one Saturday, I was assigned a bride. I knew her name, her groom's name, the time of the sealing, and the room in which they would be sealed. I sat with three other temple workers who were also awaiting brides.

Soon a lovely bride walked with her parents and fiancé to the recommend desk. The temple worker at the recommend desk told them the first step was to go to the desk across the room, where we were waiting to check in her wedding dress. When they turned around, they saw someone in the adjoining temple view room, where guests without temple recommends wait. Who they saw I do not know, but I saw their reaction. The bride and her mother burst into tears, not tears of joy but of dismay, perhaps even anger. I read the bride's lips, "Why would he do this to me on my wedding day?" It was a tense moment, but finally, with fresh tears still on their cheeks, the mother and bride made their way over to the desk.

Usually, the first thing the desk coordinator does is ask the bride her name so that the waiting temple workers know if she is "their" bride, but this time she didn't. The first words out of her mouth were, "You're in the temple. Everything is going to be fine." At the same moment, I went over to her, smiled, and took the heavy wedding dress and other items from her arms. Another temple worker had stood up with me. She walked over to the bride and gave her a kiss on the cheek.

I immediately thought about love languages and how, without thought or plan, three temple workers, I believe acting under inspiration from the Holy Ghost, had responded to a tearful bride in three different ways. The coordinator had given her words of affirmation. I provided an act of service, and the other worker gave her physical touch.

It's a beautiful experience to speak someone's love language in order to communicate more tenderly and effectively, whether in affirming words, open-ended time, thoughtful gifts, appropriate touch, acts of service, or in any combination. Under the direction of the Spirit, we can become fluent in many love languages.

Chapter 24

Are You Emotionally Stingy or Generous?

Scrooge, the Grinch who stole Christmas, and Cinderella's stepmother are extreme fictitious examples of emotionally stingy people. The emotionally stingy have strained family relationships, make poor employees, and cheat themselves out of a rewarding, happy life. You don't have to look far to find emotionally stingy people in real life. You might even see one when you look in the mirror.

The emotionally stingy have what Stephen Covey called "scarcity mentality." These people think there is only one pie. If someone else gets a bigger slice, there is obviously less for them. "People with a Scarcity Mentality have a very difficult time sharing recognition and credit, power or profit—even with those who help in the production. They also have a very hard time being genuinely happy for the successes of other people—even, and sometimes especially, members of their own family or close friends and associates."[35] People who believe there is not enough to go around forget the Lord said, "For the earth is full, and there is enough and to spare; yea, I prepared all things, and have given unto the children of men" (D&C 104:17). Scarcity mentality folks are unrealistically competitive and see other people as threats.

The emotionally stingy can be drama kings and queens who suck energy from others. They use events—no matter how insignificant—as opportunities to make life all about them. They exaggerate their moods and exploit others to keep themselves the focus of attention. These people keep relationships on the rocks, living life like a soap opera in states of depression, elation, anxiety, or turbulence.

The emotionally stingy are selfish and miserly with money, time, compliments, and commitment except with people in their circle—their

---

35 Stephen R. Covey, *The 7 Habits of Highly Effective People*, New York: Simon and Schuster, 1989, 219.

clique, their family, their friends. They are selective as to with whom they will associate. Unless they will benefit from doing what is expected, they will do just enough to get by or to look good. They are judgmental, critical, and experts at faultfinding. They view themselves as better than they are and judge others by this inflated and unrealistic view of themselves.

The emotionally stingy avoid social situations because they are uncomfortable in the normal give-and-take required in social interactions. They may concoct reasons to leave early, not attend, or dominate conversations.

The emotionally stingy often have undercurrents of anger and negativity. Fear may be their overriding emotion. They have memories of people who have offended them in the past, which proves to them that people are indeed threats.

Emotionally stingy persons are the human equivalent of a desert, almost never providing fellow travelers with water or shade or protection because "you can't draw water from an empty well," and the emotionally stingy are like raisins, shriveled up in their own needs they can't satisfy.

Celestine Chau said, "I have come across emotionally stingy people in my life, and the truth is these people just aren't very enjoyable to be around. Being around them feels like being in an emotional vortex that just sucks up all your energy and leaves you with a dry and unpleasant feeling inside. It's very draining."[36]

As uncomfortable and draining as it is to be around the emotionally stingy, it's exactly the opposite to be around emotionally generous people who have an abundance mentality, who believe there's always enough to go around and always room for one more.

Emotionally generous people focus on individuals. Emotionally generous people are committed to sharing their energy, time, resources, and selves. They see and appreciate the efforts of others. When problems arise, they discuss ways to resolve them in open, affable, and honest ways. They want to be part of the solution and bring about the greatest good. They are happy for your successes and good fortune. They actually seek the welfare of others. They listen. They don't try to control or dominate.

The emotionally generous enjoy being with people. They make and keep friends because they understand friendship is caring about others.

---

36 "Are You Emotionally Generous?" Personal Excellence, www.personalexcellence. co/blog/are-you-emotionally-generous.

They share and help; they cultivate happiness; they love; they smile; they praise; they express gratitude; they do good without expectation of receiving in return; they serve; they validate others. They also include themselves on the list of people to whom they should be emotionally generous.

Brother Johnson, a seminary teacher for the Church, spent a year being ill. He'd get well enough to go back to work for a few days and then would be sick again. He wondered many times why his boss hadn't let him go. Finally, he was able to return to work. At the first faculty meeting upon his return, Brother Johnson thanked everyone, especially his boss, who had made it possible for him to keep his job. Then Brother Johnson told this story:

"When Ezra Taft Benson was the prophet, he expressed his concern to the Twelve Apostles and said something such as, 'Most of you are very old men. Please be careful in your travels, eat wisely, and get enough sleep.' The oldest Apostle at the time, LeGrand Richards, spoke up and said, 'You are a good daddy.'" Brother Johnson had intended to say to his boss, "You are a good daddy," but his heart was too full to speak.

The emotionally generous are like good daddies and mommies. Their concern for others is genuine. You truly matter to them. Knowing you truly matter to someone is one of life's sweetest gifts—like a caress that comforts, calms, cheers, consoles, and encourages all in the same moment. Emotionally generous people understand that life is hard for everyone and go about in their unassuming and natural way to love and give in word and deed.

Chapter 25

"GIVE, THEN, AS JESUS GIVES"

"GIVE SAID THE LITTLE STREAM" has been a very popular Primary song for decades because of its catchy tune and simple rhymes. It's a happy song about singing and giving and a little stream that makes the grass grow greener. The second verse is about rain that helps droopy flowers raise their heads. Probably neither verse makes sense to children. Surely the symbolism is lost on them. The profound message only comes in the third verse. The song is about Jesus Christ and states, "Give, then, as Jesus gives" ("Give Said the Little Stream," *Children's Songbook*, 236).

Jesus taught a lesson about giving by drawing His disciples' attention to an unfolding situation. "And Jesus sat over against the treasury, and beheld how the people cast money into the treasury: and many that were rich cast in much. And there came a certain poor widow, and she threw in two mites, which make a farthing. And he called unto him his disciples, and saith unto them, Verily I say unto you, That this poor widow hath cast more in, than all they which have cast into the treasury: For all they did cast in of their abundance; but she of her want did cast in all that she had, even all her living" (Mark 12:41–44).

Latter-day Saints of today give in similar ways. It's our nature and one of the qualities that defines this Church, which bears the name of Jesus Christ. Both men and women give openly, freely, generously, and quietly, without drawing attention to their deeds.

A couple in their late twenties goes several times a month to the temple to participate in sacred ordinances. This couple got married a few years ago. In their love and testimonies, they are much like other young couples who find joy in temple service; however, this couple is unique because both of them were born with cerebral palsy. The husband walks and talks haltingly, and his wife uses a walker. Her speech is slow and deliberate.

Since neither of them can drive, they get to the temple by bus. The temple workers deeply admire this couple and feel privileged to observe their faithful temple service.

One evening, a husband and wife who from time to time help this couple in the temple, entered a restaurant to have dinner. Much to their surprise they saw their friends, the couple with cerebral palsy, also having dinner there. They went over to the table, and the two couples exchanged pleasantries. Then the waiter came and guided them to a table at the other end of the restaurant. They ordered their meal, ate, and were preparing to leave when the manager came to their table. They wondered why the manager would come talk to them when they had just asked the waiter for the check. The manager said, "The handicapped couple paid for your dinner."

"Give, then, as Jesus gives."

Jesus commands that we give to enemies as well as friends. My daughter Michelle knows what it means to "bless them that curse you, do good to them that hate you, and pray for them which despitefully use you, and persecute you" (Matthew 5:44).

She and her husband were standing at a busy intersection in Glendale, California, in October 2008, holding signs that read: "Vote *Yes* on Prop 8." They were there defending traditional marriage and defining marriage as prophets and Apostles declared. Of her experience, Michelle wrote:

> After a while, a man joined us, carrying a huge, hand-written poster with "No on Prop 8 (hate)" on one side and "Don't Support Bigotry" on the other side. He crossed each of the four crosswalks in turn, circling the intersection.
>
> As he waited on our corner he taunted, "Haters! Bigots!" I smiled patiently, but my smile only upset him more.
>
> I was smiling on the outside, but inside I prayed for a way to show him that my "*Yes* on Prop 8" sign did not represent hate. To the contrary, I felt great compassion for him, as I do for all those personally affected by this issue.
>
> A woman approached and said, "Look at me. I want you to look at me." She pointed to another woman standing nearby. "This is my partner." She pointed to two teenage girls. "These are my children. What do you say to *that*?"
>
> My husband responded, "Then you'll probably want to vote no on 8."

"You bet I will!" she replied.

The man with the *No* poster was standing nearby. The woman turned to him and asked if he needed anything. He mentioned he was hot and thirsty.

On impulse, I pulled an extra water bottle from my bag and handed it to him. He accepted it gratefully, and the woman turned to me, amazed. She said to me, intently and directly, "That was a very nice thing to do." Then, as an aside to the people with her, she said, with surprise in her voice, "She's a giver."

I watched to see if the man with the poster would drink from the water bottle. He did. When it was time for us to go, my husband and I crossed the street to talk to him. He told us about his experience living in a foreign country where, he said, you could never protest on the street.

I remarked, "Isn't it wonderful that we can stand here holding our signs with different opinions, peacefully? This is so America!" He agreed and thanked me again for the water bottle.

"I hope you know we're not haters," I earnestly told him.

He conceded, "I guess I was just really angry when I first arrived."

The giving of the water had softened the hearts of the man who was thirsty and the woman who had been so angry.

Jesus set a high standard for giving. He expects us to give our mites, be they few or many, to the Church to care for the poor. He expects that even though we may have great personal needs, the command to give is the same. He expects us to give our water bottles to people who are calling us derogatory names.

Jesus knows all about giving. He gives us mercy, more than we deserve. He gives the equivalent of the widow's mite and more. He condescended and gave up the comforts and nobility of heavenly realms to teach, heal, rescue, and more. He gave His perfect life to be abused and crucified with criminals. He is the ultimate giver and admonishes, "Go, and do thou likewise" (Luke 10:37). "Give, then, as Jesus gives."

Chapter 26

HELPING TO SAVE SOULS

I was working in a room with my back to a double glass door. Suddenly, out of the corner of my eye, I saw something hit the glass and heard a little thud followed almost immediately by a loud thud. I looked out the window and saw a bird about twenty inches long on its back. Its wings, which would measure thirty inches from wingtip to wingtip, were lying limply open out to the sides. The bird, I had no idea what kind it was, had obviously crashed at high speed into the glass. Its chest was heaving, and its beak opened every few seconds, gasping for air. I knew it would be dead soon. I opened the glass door with the idea that I'd get a shovel from the shed and dig a grave for it. But to my surprise, when I opened the door, on the threshold was a beautiful black-and-yellow finch with a broken neck. I realized what had happened. The bigger bird, a predator, was so focused on having finch for lunch, and the finch so concerned about being lunch, that they both missed the fact that what looked like sky was actually a glass door.

I got a shovel and dug a little grave for the finch. Then I used my foot to carefully roll the little body onto the shovel. I studied its elegant black-and-yellow pattern and took a few moments to acknowledge the Creator of this little creature and buried it. Then I walked back to see if the bigger bird was dead yet. It was still gasping, so I gently used my foot to fold first one wing and then the other wing close to its body. The craftsmanship of the wings was exquisite. Each feather fit in length and color precisely with the ones on either side. The feathers made a slight rustling sound when moved. Then I gently moved the bird with my foot onto the shovel and rolled it onto its belly. As I did, I saw its spectacular markings of browns, grays, black, and white align precisely with the tail markings. I moved it on the shovel, walked to a protected spot in the yard, and gently laid it on the ground. Then the thought occurred to get some water.

I went into the house, took the cap off a gallon of milk, and filled it with water. I went back outside and put the cap of water next to the bird's beak. It didn't move at all. I studied it, realizing this was a rare and intimate moment. After a few minutes of awe-filled observation, I returned to the house, planning to come back and bury it later.

About an hour later, my son Dan, who is an outdoorsman, came home. I told him the story. He excitedly went to where the bird was as I watched from the doorway. When he got to the spot, he looked down at the bird then back at me and exclaimed, "Mom, it's a peregrine—" He almost got "falcon" out when the bird suddenly spread its mighty, aerodynamic wings and, with a few flaps, was out of sight. I went out and looked at the cap of water. It was empty. I wrote in my journal: "Today I had the privilege of saving a peregrine falcon." I felt deep-down joy at the privilege of helping to save one of God's creatures.

Reporting on his mission, an Elder Dixon told of the circumstances when he found the most wonderful convert of his whole mission, when he knew he had saved a soul. He said he and his companion were riding their bikes on a cold, damp day in Portland, Oregon. They were on their way to follow up on a referral. He was new to the area and saw they had to climb a long, steep hill. Suddenly the clouds opened up, and they were caught in a downpour. Quickly taking shelter under an awning, they put on their rain gear. Elder Dixon had grown up in Dallas, Texas, and the Portland weather was wearing him down. He thought, *I'm sick of gray, gloomy skies, and RAIN.* But he said nothing and continued to pedal through the storm. When he realized they were less than a block from their apartment, he wanted to go home and wait out the storm. It wasn't as though they had an appointment. They could check out this referral tomorrow, next week, or even next month. But his companion kept pedaling toward the hill.

Well, Elder Dixon thought, trying to console himself, *perhaps this is going to be one of those amazing stories that, despite rain, wind, and fatigue, the missionaries kept moving forward toward their goal and were rewarded with the most wonderful convert of their missions.* So he kept pedaling. Finally, they got to the top of the hill and began looking for the address. After several tries, they found the house. Elder Dixon knocked on the door. A man answered and told them if they ever came to his door again, he'd call the police.

As they rode back down the hill, Elder Dixon expected to feel dejected, but instead he felt a sense of comfort. Despite being cold and soaked to the skin, a feeling of warmth began to fill his heart. The feeling grew until he knew as never before that Heavenly Father loved him, that he was serving as an ambassador of Jesus Christ, and that his efforts were ratified and accepted by Them. Basking in the sunlight of the Spirit, a scripture came into his mind: "And if it so be that you should labor all your days in crying repentance unto this people, and bring, save it be one soul unto me, how great shall be your joy with him in the kingdom of my Father!" (D&C 18:15). He knew he'd just been blessed with his most important convert of his whole mission—himself—and his joy was full.

What joy awaits when you are privileged to help save the soul of any of Father in Heaven's creations—children, family, friends, but especially and most critically, yourself.

Chapter 27

HOSPITAL WARDS AND LDS WARDS

THE TERM *HOSPITAL WARD* DESIGNATES a section of the hospital shared by patients with similar needs. Everyone in a hospital ward is ill and has come to be treated. Doctors oversee the care of each patient. There are nurses who attend to individual needs and carry out doctors' orders.

Unlike most other churches, members of The Church of Jesus Christ of Latter-day Saints don't choose which congregation to attend. The geographic area in which a member lives determines his or her ward. The number of people in a hospital ward is few compared to an LDS ward, but there are parallels.

Like people in a hospital ward, everyone in an LDS ward has similar needs. Everyone in both kinds of wards has infirmities. Everyone is striving to get better—physically, mentally, emotionally, socially, and spiritually. There is a bishop who, like the chief doctor, oversees the care given to each person. There are other doctors with specialties. For example, there are Primary workers who are like pediatricians—they care for children. There are home and visiting teachers who are like nurses, assessing needs and caring for individuals, one-on-one, carrying out the doctor's (bishop's) instructions. In both kinds of wards, there are clerks who keep track of each person's progress.

The most important element in both kinds of wards is that one ward member doesn't inflict harm on another because they're all neighbors. A person in a hospital ward doesn't steal medicine from another patient, stop an IV from flowing, or tell the doctors or nurses untruths about other patients. Neither should neighbors cause harm to each other, members or not. "Now there was a strict law among the people of the church, that there should not any man, belonging to the church, arise and persecute those that did not belong to the church, and that there should be no persecution among themselves" (Alma 1:21). Neighbors, like doctors, should live the Hippocratic oath: "Do no harm." Jesus Christ's teachings about neighbors is simple: "Love one another."

Examples of Christlike living abound in wards. A family needs a new roof; neighbors help. Families move in or out; neighbors help. When there's a death, a birth, a job loss, a joyful event, neighbors come, share, care, and support. Neighbors help each other and look out for their common interests. Neighbors do the right thing.

Two neighbors, Bill and Dave, both thought they owned a strip of ground between their two homes. Dave put in a sprinkling system and a fence. Bill felt betrayed but fumed in silence. Dave planted trees and flowers, built a tree house, and had a trampoline installed. With each addition, Bill felt more wronged. Five years passed, and Bill researched the titles and confirmed that he actually owned the strip of ground. When Bill showed his neighbor the evidence, Dave didn't want to give it up. He said he had invested too much and that it was too late to do anything about it. Bill got an attorney. The wives stopped speaking. The children felt animosity toward the other's family.

Fortunately, this territorial skirmish has a happy conclusion. Dave and his wife realized how shortsighted and unchristian their actions had been. In humility, they went to Bill's home, checkbook in hand, apologized for their actions, and offered to pay full value for the strip of land. Bill and his wife accepted the offer.

We lived next door to Lester, Karen, and their daughter for twenty years. During the most active time in our family, they were approaching or enjoying retirement. We had eight young children. Balls from our yard continually ended up in their yard. Three different times, balls from our yard broke windows in their house. We had a barking dog; they didn't. They went to bed early; we didn't. One day I was working out back and noticed Lester digging a big hole beside the fence that divided our yards. I asked what he was doing. He said, "I'm planting us a peach tree." He planted it on the property line so that both families could enjoy the fruit! Every year I'd get a phone call: "This is Lester. Your peaches are ripe." The duty of neighbors is to bless each others' lives.

Similarly, a Latter-day Saint ward is a unit of society, a group of people who live in a defined geographic area. You buy a house or move into an apartment; you live in that ward. Those people become your neighbors, and the Lord commands, "Love thy neighbor as thyself" (Matthew 19:19), and "This is my commandment, That ye love one another, as I have loved you" (John 15:12).

Chapter 28

THE PERFECTION MYTH DEBUNKED

HAVE YOU EVER FELT CONFLICTED by the scripture, "Be ye therefore perfect even as your Father which is in heaven is perfect" (Matthew 5:48)? The conflict comes because you believe the scriptures are the word of God, but you know you can't be perfect. Worse than making you feel conflicted, does the word *perfect* throw you into a spiritual panic attack? Does *perfect* make you feel inadequate because you assume there are perfect people out there but that you just aren't one of them? At some point have you realized you can't be perfect at anything let alone everything? All the above presents a dilemma for too many women in the Church who feel stress and pressure to be perfect. If you have ever been a victim of the perfection myth, prepare yourself for a wonderful surprise because the perfection myth is about to be debunked.

Women threatened by the word *perfect* assume it means "without flaw." If *perfect*, as a gospel term means "without flaw," you can't be perfect because if you had only committed one sin or made one mistake in your whole life, it is one too many. You have sinned and therefore can't be perfect.

The truth is Heavenly Father knows you can't be perfect if perfect means flawless. Here is the evidence. Why would He provide a Savior to redeem you if you could be perfect on your own? Perfect people don't need a Savior. Happily, individual perfection is not part of Heavenly Father's plan for us right now. We cannot perfect ourselves, but we can be perfect in acknowledging we need a Savior, and ultimately we can be perfected in Him! (See 1 John 2:5, Moroni 10:32.)

Do you remember the people in the Book of Mormon who buried their weapons? These people, the people of Ammon, are described as "perfectly honest and upright in all things; and they were firm in the faith of Christ" (Alma 27:27). Did they still make mistakes? Of course.

Did they fall short of being flawless? Of course, like the rest of us. But the scripture still describes them as "perfect" because they were firm in the faith of Christ.

Another evidence. In 2 Nephi, Lehi is giving a blessing to his son Jacob: "And now, Jacob . . . thy soul shall be blessed, and thou shalt dwell safely with thy brother, Nephi; and thy days shall be spent in the service of thy God. Wherefore, I know that thou art redeemed, because of the righteousness of . . ." Do you think that Jacob is being promised that he will be redeemed because of *his* righteousness? Not so. Jacob will become a great prophet; he will see the Savior, but his righteousness won't save him. Finishing the sentence, "Wherefore, I know that thou art redeemed, because of the righteousness of thy Redeemer" (2 Nephi 2:3). It is because of Jesus Christ's righteousness that we are redeemed.

Another evidence. The sacrament prayer on the bread tells us we don't have to be perfect: "O God, the Eternal Father, we ask thee in the name of thy Son, Jesus Christ, to bless and sanctify this bread to the souls of all those who partake of it, that they may eat in remembrance of the body of thy Son, and witness unto thee, O God, the Eternal Father, that they are *willing*"—if the word *willing* was not there, we would be covenanting to be perfect because the rest of the prayer says—"to take upon them the name of thy Son, and always remember him and keep his commandments which he has given them" (D&C 20:77, emphasis added). We covenant to be willing, not to be perfect. And when we are *willing*, we receive the greatest of gifts to help us be better than our flawed selves would otherwise be. As you know, the prayer ends, "That they may always have his Spirit [the Holy Ghost] to be with them" (D&C 20:77). With that Spirit we can be better than we were, but still not perfect.

Let's look at another evidence. In "The Living Christ," the testimony issued by the First Presidency and the Twelve Apostles on January 1, 2000, the next to last paragraph reads, "Each of us will stand to be judged of Him according to our works and the *desires* of our hearts" (emphasis added). Isn't this wonderful? We will be judged by our desires too.

If you pronounce *perfect*, with the stress on the last syllable, it becomes a verb that means "to improve." Striving to improve is something we all can do. Alexander Pope said, "No one should be ashamed to admit they are wrong, which is but saying, in other words, that they are wiser today than they were yesterday."[37]

---

37 Quotations Book, quotationsbook.com/quote/19798/#sthash.W1MTI6t0.dpbs.

Instead of focusing on how "imperfect" you feel, turn it about and focus on being worthy. Worthiness is an achievable standard—worthy to partake of the sacrament, worthy to have callings, worthy to attend the temple. With this beautiful desire, in the timing of the Lord, you will ultimately achieve perfection as you "Come unto Christ, and [are] perfected in him" (Moroni 10:32).

Chapter 29

THE ROAD YOU'RE ON WILL TAKE YOU WHERE IT GOES

WHEN I WAS ABOUT SEVEN, I asked my father where our street began and ended. Being an educator, he seized the moment and told me to get in the car. He drove to where our road ended, turned the car around, and drove to where it began.

From this experience I learned you could only get to my house if you are on Fifth East. You could drive up and down Fourth East or Sixth East forever and never come to my house. I learned the road you are on will take you where the road goes and nowhere else, and as a corollary, if the road you are on is not taking you where you want to end up, you need to get off that road now.

This concept, although very elementary, is one of the most critical lessons of life. If you want to graduate from high school, you have to get on the graduate-from-high-school road, obey the rules of that road (fulfil the requirements), and follow that road until it ends. If you do, you'll not only graduate from high school but will discover that a high school diploma opens up many new roads. If you want to have a healthier body, you have to find and stay on that road, which means obeying the rules of eating and exercise.

On the other hand, if you think you're a good member of the Church but begin to criticize the prophet, read anti-Mormon blogs, become lax in your prayers, scripture study, and temple attendance, you may not even be able to pinpoint the moment you lose the Spirit and start down Apostate Avenue, a road you never intended to take. You may think you are traveling on Happily-Married Boulevard, but if you criticize your spouse, compare him/her to a past flame, show disrespect to his/her ideas, or spend a lot of money without consulting him/her, you may one day realize you are traveling alone on Divorce Drive.

Faithful members of the Church sometimes worry if they will make it to the celestial kingdom. The answer is yes, of course they will, if they are on that road. If they are on Great and Spacious Boulevard, however, they'll find it is a well-paved road to somewhere else. It seems wise to get on the road and stay on the road that will take you where you want your final destination to be.

Richard and I were on a road trip from Arcata, California, to our home in Salt Lake City. We could take California 101 to tie in with Interstate 80, which our GPS said would take 302 minutes, or we could take a shortcut on Highway 299 to Redding and eventually to Interstate 5—only 140 minutes. We did the math and figured that by taking the "shortcut," we would be traveling about 50 miles per hour, and any road you can go 50 miles per hour on can't be that bad. Right?

I wish I'd charted the elevation changes—sea level to over 5,000 feet, up one mountainside and down another. Then there were construction zones, delays, and one-lane roads. It took over four hours, which was more like 35 miles per hour! Yes, you are thinking, but you saw so much more than if you'd been on the freeway. Not really, and it was anything but relaxing as road signs kept warning of obstacles and hazards—deer, rock slides, turnouts, construction vehicles reentering the road, one-lane traffic, when and when not to pass. The choice to take 299 greatly increased our risk of accident.

I should have studied the options before embarking or asked someone who knew the area. My suppositions that a shorter route would be faster and equally safe were errors in judgment.

At Hampton Court, England, there is a famous maze with high, well-manicured hedges covering a half mile of paths on a third of an acre. Everyone gets lost in it. When you become frustratingly lost, a man who is perched in a tower high above the maze—a guard whose job is to stand and keep watch—will direct you safely out of the maze.

There is a sentinel who can spare you the agony of taking a wrong road. If you listen to this man, you will be protected from the mistakes, errors, and sins of a dead-end road. You can save yourself from becoming physically or spiritually lost and from having to suffer the consequences of dangerous roads. The sentinel who has the view above the maze of life, who has been placed in a position above the rest of humanity, is the prophet, seer, and revelator of The Church of Jesus Christ of Latter-day Saints. If you follow his counsel, you will avoid forbidden paths and arrive safely at your destination.

Chapter 30

CHILDREN AND CHORES

It's Saturday morning, and Kevin is just finishing breakfast with his eleven-year-old son, Spencer. Kevin tells Spencer they'll go on a hike as soon as the boy's chores are done. "Dad, I'm almost done. I folded some laundry and weeded my section of the garden. All I have to do is clean my room." With that Spencer gulps down a last bite of toast with some orange juice and runs off to clean his room.

"Isn't he a great kid," Kevin proudly says to his wife, who has just entered the room. Almost before she has a chance to respond, Spencer is back.

"I'm ready to go, Dad."

"Really?" says Kevin. "That's the fastest room-cleaning on record. Well, let's grab a couple granola bars and some bottled water and be on our way." Then a thought crosses Kevin's mind. "Spencer, I think I'd like to see the results of the fastest room-cleaning in history." With Spencer leading the way, Kevin enters Spencer's room and looks around to see clothes hanging out of half-open drawers. Lego pieces, papers, and books cover the desk and floor. The bedcovers are pulled up on an angle with the pillow recklessly tossed on top. "Spencer, I wouldn't call this room clean," Kevin says in a disappointed voice.

"Oh, don't worry, Dad," Spencer replies cheerfully. "Mom always fixes it."

Good parenting is walking a fine line between being lenient—always fixing it—and being austere—never fixing it. Mothers especially have difficulty making such decisions. Should she take her son's forgotten lunch to school, or should she let him experience the consequences of forgetting the lunch, knowing that missing one meal won't hurt him and might even help him be more responsible? Should she wash her daughter's dirty, smelly uniform because she likes to be helpful and kind, or should she let the child's coach or teammates tell the girl that the uniform is not presentable and that it stinks?

Since mothers' natural instincts are to love and serve, fixing comes naturally. Not fixing things is hard. It is heart wrenching to watch the consequences that follow a child's poor choices play out. Mothers know, however, that bailing a child out of cleaning his room, taking a forgotten lunch to school, and washing that uniform aren't necessarily loving and serving. Doing for a child what he should do for himself may cause him to think that he'll always be rescued from the responsibilities of life. When a parent enables a child to continue in bad behavior, the child fails to progress toward adulthood. Mothers need to simply say, "I'm sorry you forgot your lunch," and leave it at that.

I have struggled with this delicate balance between being too permissive and too strict since my first child was eight months old and wouldn't sleep through the night. I wondered, do I just let him cry it out, or do I continue to respond to his cries? Even with adult children, I don't want to assume responsibility that rightfully belongs to them. Knowing when to help and when to stand by and pray is very difficult. And in grandparenting, the dilemma is still there.

One of my adult sons called me, explaining that his wife was at a doctor's appointment, that he was going into a mandatory meeting at work, and that nine-year-old Sammy had just called from school saying he was sick. Could I go pick him up?

When I got to the school, I put my hand on Sammy's forehead. He didn't have a fever. He said, "Thank you for coming to get me, Grandma. My stomach hurts."

"I'm sorry," I said, watching him slowly put on his backpack and walk painfully slowly down the hall.

When we got in the car, he asked me what we were going to do when we got home. I told him I needed to vacuum the car, and he asked if he could help. He worked beside me, wiping down the interior of the car with a damp cloth while I vacuumed. When that was finished, he asked if I would play a game of chess with him. You can see my dilemma. Should I have said, "No, Sammy, you came home from school because you said you were sick. You need to go lie down until your dad comes to get you," or should I have left the consequences of faking sickness to his parents?

When to bail a child out and when to let him learn through experience is a hard call. Parenting by prayer under the direction of the

Spirit is the only way that really works long term because I never knew (know) when the child had tried hard enough, worked long enough, or was truly sick. The Spirit will help us learn to let natural consequences happen. Allowing uncomfortable results to follow bad behavior is a profound teacher. The Spirit will also help us know when to impose consequences—punishments.

Spencer's mother felt she had been too lenient with her son, so she went to the Internet to find a list of age-appropriate chores. On the Focus on the Family website, she saw a list of chores by age. "Aha." She smiled to herself as she read the list. "Age 8 to 11—keep bedroom clean!" Then she experienced a sudden flash of inspiration: *I won't be there to make Kevin's room look presentable when he's off to college, on a mission, or even worse, married. My job is to prepare him for adulthood.* A plan started forming in her mind whereby she would help Spencer learn life skills. She thought of three categories: ways Spencer could contribute to the upkeep of the home, ways Spencer should take responsibility for his own life and possessions, and ways Spencer could increase in personal hygiene, good manners, and gratitude.

When Adam and Eve were expelled from the Garden of Eden, God told Adam he would have to work: "By the sweat of thy face shalt thou eat bread" (Moses 4:25). God Himself knows the hard work of planning, creating, and maintaining. His glory is to teach others to achieve His level of work and glory.

Children need to be taught that success comes on the heels of hard work and that rest comes after strenuous labor. The earlier they learn to "put their shoulder to the wheel" the better. Working together as a family where everyone shares in chores is the ideal training ground. The motto is, "If you live here, you work here." The basic housework has to be done, and everyone is responsible to do his or her share. Children who are willing to do extra jobs can be paid for their initiative. The earlier a child correlates the connection between money and work, the better money manager he or she will become.

Children need to learn that money, self-respect, confidence, and independence come as natural consequences from doing a job well, not from a mother who always fixes the problems.

Chapter 31

SCRIPTURE STUDY—THEME AND VARIATIONS

How OFTEN HAVE YOU HEARD the admonition to study the scriptures? Probably every week someone in some meeting mentions the need for and blessings of scripture study. Scripture study is the theme, but we each have our own system or method to make the scriptures part of our lives. Some of these variations follow:

A Primary teacher gave each child in her class a three-minute timer and challenged them to read the Book of Mormon at least that long each day.

A young mother reads scripture daily as she blow-dries her long, thick hair. Another listens to the Book of Mormon online (see http://lds.org/broadcast/scriptures/0,5393,48-1,00.html) as she gets ready for the day.

One family places a Book of Mormon on a chair before dinner. The person who sits in that chair reads a few verses aloud to the family before they start to eat.

One husband and wife take turns reading a chapter of scripture aloud every night together.

Some study scripture by topic from the Topical Guide.

Some underline.

Some make notes in the margins.

Some read cover to cover.

Some read out of order.

Some mark scriptures according to subject.

Some mark scriptures per instruction like at http://scripturemarking.com/index.html.

Some prefer not to mark their scriptures so new ideas and inspiration can come.

Some listen as they exercise.

Some listen as they commute.

Some read in the language of their mission to keep up language skills and gain added insights.

Some memorize favorite passages.

Some think reading the Bible Dictionary is the best way to learn the interconnectedness of scripture.

Thousands of seminary students memorize the scripture mastery scriptures. (See http://seminary.lds.org/mastery/ for a complete list and helpful resources.) Some sign up to receive a daily scripture mastery scripture by e-mail.

Some read scriptures online at http://lds.org/scriptures?lang=eng.

Some prefer reading with the leather between their hands; some read on electronic devices; the blind read with their fingers at http://lds.org/braille/0,18908,5388-1,00.html.

Some young children learn scripture stories from colorfully illustrated books: *New Testament Stories, Old Testament Stories, Book of Mormon Stories,* and *Doctrine and Covenants Stories.* These come in a variety of media formats—downloadable text, audio, video, and American Sign (ASL). You can buy the stories as books or as a DVD set at a distribution center. You can also order them online at http://store.lds.org/webapp/wcs/stores/servlet/TopCategories1_10705_10551_-1.

Some families listen to the new Scripture Stories Radio Series on the Mormon Radio Channel. Each episode features children sharing their insights and favorite experiences from the scriptures, accompanied by music and reading from the scriptures: http://radio.lds.org/eng/programs/scripture-stories.

Some families post scriptures on doorways and on walls of their homes. In the Church offices in downtown Salt Lake City, a quote from general conference or from the scriptures is posted in every elevator to "elevate your thoughts."

Some, from time to time, study scripture randomly, letting a book of scripture fall open and reading where their eyes first fall.

Reading charts appeal to some. There are many options online. One ten-minute-a-day reading chart can be found in the *Book of Mormon Student Study Guide*, page 7.

Some read a specific number of pages each day or just read until they find a passage to ponder for the rest of the day.

Some keep lists of personal favorites—scriptures that are especially sweet and meaningful. Then when something sad or bad happens, the list is immediately available. You can add to your list as you find new favorites.

A widow wanted to leave her children a tangible spiritual legacy. She prayed for an idea. The idea came to handwrite the entire Book of Mormon and have it copied and bound for each of them. Writing involves additional senses and increases retention.

Jesus said, "He that hath the scriptures, let him search them" (3 Nephi 10:14). With all the technological helps available today, we will have a hard time explaining to Him why we didn't search the scriptures as He commanded.

Every aspect of life is enhanced by reading, searching, pondering, and praying about the scriptures. In the scriptures, the words of Christ are conveyed into the hearts of readers by the power of the Holy Ghost. "Wherefore, I said unto you, feast upon the words of Christ; for behold, the words of Christ will tell you all things what ye should do" (2 Nephi 32:3).

Chapter 32

ANTICIPATING YOUR RESURRECTION

As you know, no one gets out of this life alive. Every person will die. Physical bodies are placed in graves or urns, and spirit bodies "are taken home to that God who gave them life" (Alma 40:11). Some confuse this process and think the spirit body returning to God is the Resurrection. Not so. Others are confused about why the body and spirit need to come back together. Alma's son Corianton was concerned about the Resurrection. Alma said to him, "Now my son, . . . I perceive that thy mind is worried concerning the resurrection of the dead" (Alma 40:1). With the knowledge the restored gospel provides, death and resurrection are better understood.

Right now, with our spirits and bodies joined, we don't feel the great need for the Resurrection because we don't realize what it is like to be only a spirit. When we are dead, however, we will want our bodies back. The scriptures confirm this: "The dead [look] upon the long absence of their spirits from their bodies as a bondage" (D&C 138:50).

If you're still wondering why even a glorified, resurrected body is better than a spirit body, the scriptures clarify this. "The elements are eternal, and spirit and element, inseparably connected, receive a fulness of joy; and when separated, man cannot receive a fulness of joy" (D&C 93:33–34).

The scriptures are clear on why you cannot progress and obtain a fullness of joy without your body. If there were no Resurrection, "if the flesh should rise no more our spirits must become subject to . . . the devil . . . and we become devils, angels to a devil, to be shut out from the presence of our God" (2 Nephi 9:8–9). The Resurrection makes a fullness of joy possible because it is a protection against the devil and from being shut out from the presence of God. Also, without a resurrected body, you cannot progress beyond a certain point. That is why the resurrection is so important, so vital, so crucial.

However, we will not receive the same body back. The resurrection is the power and process whereby worn-out bodies are refurbished, refined, and glorified. You will long for that kind of a body that can never get hurt, sick, or old. A resurrected body has many capabilities of which we have yet to learn.

Resurrection means birth into a new phase of eternity.

Not only will every person who ever lived on the earth be resurrected, but animals will be resurrected and enjoy "felicity" (D&C 77:3).

How does resurrection happen? The same way birth happens—by the power of our Eternal Father and His Son Jesus Christ. Jesus said, "Therefore doth my Father love me, because I lay down my life, that I might take it again. No man taketh it from me, but I lay it down of myself. I have power to lay it down, and I have power to take it again" (John 10:17–18).

Brigham Young said resurrection is a priesthood ordinance: "It is supposed by this people that we have all the ordinances in our possession for life and salvation, and exaltation, and that we are administering in these ordinances. This is not the case. We are in possession of all the ordinances that can be administered in the flesh; but there are other ordinances and administrations that must be administered beyond this world. I know you would ask what they are. I will mention one. We have not, neither can we receive here, the ordinance and the keys of the resurrection" (*Journal of Discourses*, 15:137–38).

Jesus Christ holds the keys of death and hell (see Revelation 1:18). Before Christ there was no resurrection. By virtue of the keys He holds, He counteracts death. At His Resurrection, among the Nephites "many saints did arise" (3 Nephi 23:11), and in Israel, "the graves were opened; and many bodies of the saints which slept arose, and came out of the graves after his resurrection, and went into the holy city, and appeared unto many" (Matthew 27:52–53).

A full understanding of the resurrection hinges on the knowledge that the teachings, example, and commandments of Jesus Christ are not just about living a good life here on earth. "If in this life only we have hope in Christ, we are of all men most miserable. But now is Christ risen from the dead, and become the firstfruits of them that slept" (1 Corinthians 15:19–20). Those who believe in the resurrection of Christ and anticipate their own resurrection are filled with hope.

Resurrection occurs in stages. When Jesus Christ comes in His glory at the beginning of the Millennium, some graves will be opened. At this time, a partial judgment takes place. The wicked or unjust will have to wait longer to receive their bodies. At the First Resurrection, the bodies of the righteous or just are released from their graves. "Speaking of the resurrection of the dead, . . . [they] shall come forth; they who have done good, in the resurrection of the just; and they who have done evil, in the resurrection of the unjust" (D&C 76:16–17). We strive to be worthy of the First Resurrection.

What does a body look like when it comes out of the grave? From prophetic teachings we know that a child will still be a child. This is one of the most comforting truths of the gospel of Jesus Christ. "The child that was buried in its infancy will come up in the form of the child that it was when it was laid down; then it will begin to develop. From the day of the resurrection, the body will develop until it reaches the full measure of the stature of its spirit."[38] We know from scripture some facts about what adults will look like. Amulek taught, "The spirit and the body shall be reunited again in its perfect form; both limb and joint shall be restored to its proper frame. . . . And even there shall not so much as a hair of their heads be lost; but every thing shall be restored to its perfect frame" (Alma 11:43–44).

Resurrection liberates, restores, and makes new.

More than five hundred people in the Old World testified they saw Jesus Christ alive after He died. Mary Magdalene, other women, two disciples on the road to Emmaus, Peter, ten Apostles, eleven Apostles at Jerusalem, eleven disciples at the Sea of Galilee, eleven disciples on a mountain in Galilee, more than five hundred brethren at once, James, eleven Apostles at the Ascension, Stephen, Paul, Ananias, and John the Revelator.

Thousands more saw Him as recorded in the Book of Mormon. The prophet Mormon was fifteen when he saw Him. Moroni recorded, "And then shall ye know that I have seen Jesus, and that he hath talked with me face to face" (Ether 12:39). "I speak unto you as if ye were present, and yet ye are not. But behold, Jesus Christ hath shown you unto me" (Mormon 8:35).

In 1820, Joseph Smith saw Him in the woods not far from his log home in Palmyra, New York. In 1832, Joseph Smith and Sidney Rigdon

38 As quoted in *Latter-day Prophets Speak*, ed. by Daniel H. Ludlow, Salt Lake City: Bookcraft, 1951, 44.

saw Him as recorded in Doctrine and Covenants 76, and in 1836, Joseph Smith and Oliver Cowdery saw Him, the details of which can be read in Doctrine and Covenants 110.

At His Second Coming all the people of the earth will see Him together! "And the glory of the Lord shall be revealed, and all flesh shall see it together" (Isaiah 40:5).

It goes without saying that the fact that there is such a thing as resurrection is clear evidence that there is life after death. Eternal life is an opportunity to experience "life" in different states: as an intelligence prior to being clothed with a spirit body (Abraham 3:21–22), as a mortal, as a spirit postmortality, and as a resurrected being when spirit and body are forever "inseparably connected" (D&C 93:33).

From the state of being an intelligence to being a resurrected being, the great plan of happiness is in progress. A dying mother said to her adult daughter, "Do you believe in the plan of salvation?"

"Of course, I do. You know that I do," responded the daughter, whose grief was already acute.

"But do you believe in the plan of salvation for me?" her mother asked. The mother was asking her daughter for permission to die. She was ready for her private, personal plan of happiness to move forward. She was ready for her next stage of progression.

You may believe in the plan of salvation, but when it comes to parting with a beloved parent, spouse, or child, can you endure the separation, this greatest trial of faith? We parted at birth from those we love, and we part from those we love at death. Partings are as much a part of the plan as reunions. "Weeping may endure for a night, but joy cometh in the morning" (Psalm 30:5), the morning of the First Resurrection. "O how great the plan of our God!" (2 Nephi 9:13).

Chapter 33

THE HOLY GARMENT

MUCH CURIOSITY EXISTS ABOUT GARMENTS, the sacred underclothing members of The Church of Jesus Christ of Latter-day Saints wear after receiving their temple endowment. The word *garment* is found in scripture 91 times, and *garments* is found 133 times. Sometimes it seems to be a synonym for any clothing; other times it specifically refers to a sacred article of clothing.

From the Old Testament: "And take thou unto thee Aaron thy brother, and his sons with him, from among the children of Israel, that he may minister unto me in the priest's office. . . . And thou shalt make holy garments for Aaron" (Exodus 28:1–2). "And the priest, whom he shall anoint, and whom he shall consecrate to minister in the priest's office in his father's stead, shall make the atonement, and shall put on the linen clothes, even the holy garments" (Leviticus 16:32).

From the New Testament: "And Jesus answered . . . The kingdom of heaven is like unto a certain king, which made a marriage for his son. . . . And when the king came in to see the guests, he saw there a man which had not on a wedding garment: And he saith unto him, Friend, how camest thou in hither not having a wedding garment? And he was speechless. Then said the king to the servants, Bind him hand and foot, and take him away, and cast him into outer darkness; there shall be weeping and gnashing of teeth" (Matthew 22:1–2, 11–13). "Thou hast a few names even in Sardis which have not defiled their garments; and they shall walk with me in white: for they are worthy" (Revelation 3:4).

From the Book of Mormon: "I say unto you, ye will know at that day that ye cannot be saved; for there can no man be saved except his garments are washed white; yea, his garments must be purified until they are cleansed from all stain, through the blood of him of whom it has been spoken by our fathers, who should come to redeem his people from their sins" (Alma 5:21). "Awake, and arise from the dust, O Jerusalem; yea, and put on thy beautiful garments, O daughter of Zion" (Moroni 10:31).

From the Doctrine and Covenants: "Yea, verily I say unto you, Zion must arise and put on her beautiful garments" (D&C 82:14).

From www.mormonnewsroom.org:

> In our world of diverse religious observance, many people of faith wear special clothing as a reminder of sacred beliefs and commitments. This has been a common practice throughout history. Today, faithful adult members of The Church of Jesus Christ of Latter-day Saints wear temple garments. These garments are simple, white underclothing composed of two pieces: a top piece similar to a T-shirt and a bottom piece similar to shorts. Not unlike the Jewish *tallit katan* (prayer shawl), these garments are worn underneath regular clothes. Temple garments serve as a personal reminder of covenants made with God to lead good, honorable, Christlike lives. The wearing of temple garments is an outward expression of an inward commitment to follow the Savior.[39]

That outward expression shows an understanding of the sacred nature of the body, a body created in the image of God. "So God created man in his own image, in the image of God created he him; male and female created he them" (Genesis 1:27). The garment worn properly bespeaks of an inward desire to dress modestly according to the Lord's standard rather than the world's ever-changing fashion. "Know ye not that ye are the temple of God, and that the Spirit of God dwelleth in you?" (1 Corinthians 3:16).

The garment is as important to wear as it was to wear armor in battles of the past and as necessary as it is for police to wear bulletproof clothing today. The Apostle Paul said with authority: "Take unto you the whole armour of God, that ye may be able to withstand in the evil day" (Ephesians 6:13). Father Lehi likewise used strong language when speaking to his sons: "Awake, my sons; put on the armor of righteousness" (2 Nephi 1:23). Members of the Church who have been endowed in the

---

39 "Temple Garments," Newsroom, http://www.mormonnewsroom.org/article/ temple-garments.

holy temple likewise wear the garment as a means of protection—physically, spiritually, emotionally, and intellectually—and as a way to honor their covenants and to increase in righteousness.

Ashley and Steve had just been sealed in the temple. Ashley had worn a temple dress rather than her wedding dress so that every time she went to the temple she would be wearing the dress in which she was married. After the sealing ceremony, Ashley changed into her wedding dress, which Steve had not seen. His anticipation to see his beautiful bride in her wedding dress built as he waited for her to come out of the dressing room. Suddenly, he saw her coming toward him. The closer she got, the more his countenance changed from elation to concern. When she was standing in front of him, he put his arms around her neck and whispered, "Where are your garments?" Ashley, misunderstanding the covenant associated with wearing garments properly, had chosen a sleeveless dress with a low neckline. She had tucked in and pulled down her garments so they would not show.

You probably remember the story of three men who were applying for a job with a trucking company. The interviewer told the men that the route they would drive was dangerous, over high, narrow mountain roads. Each man was asked about his driving skills. The first said he was experienced in driving long-haul big rigs and could get to the very edge of the cliff and maintain control of the truck. The second said he could keep control even if part of the tires were off the edge. The third said his philosophy was to drive as far from the edge as possible.

Wearing temple garments is a similar dilemma for some. The only safe way is to choose clothing that covers the holy garment to avoid getting close to the edge.

Find joy in wearing the garment rather than looking for excuses not to wear it. Only then will the promised blessings come. We can't always be in the temple, but we can always have part of the temple with us.

Chapter 34

YEARNING TO BE UNDERSTOOD

AN ADORABLE EIGHTEEN-MONTH-OLD CAN ONLY SAY a few words clearly. Everything else he jabbers in his own language. His mother tries hard to understand him, especially when his need seems urgent. "Do you want a drink?" "Do you want Daddy?" "Do you want your blanket?" When she guesses wrong, he becomes frustrated and shakes his head over and over again until she gets it right. Then he nods happily. It feels good to be understood.

A couple who married on Christmas Eve stopped at a grocery store to purchase food for the next few days, which they would spend at a condo for their honeymoon. The husband put chocolate chips, flour, baking soda, sugar, butter, and pecans in the shopping cart. The wife, though very much in love and very happy to be married, was thinking about the traditional Christmas Eve her parents and siblings were having. Although her husband encouraged her to put items she wanted in the cart, all she wanted was pumpkin pie—her family's traditional Christmas Eve dessert.

When they arrived at the honeymoon place, she started putting the food away. He found a mixing bowl and took out a recipe from his pocket. When she realized what he was doing, tears leaked onto her cheek. He looked at her in questioning bewilderment.

Finally, she asked, "Aren't you missing what you've done all of your life on Christmas Eve? Aren't you thinking at all about what your family is doing right now?"

"Yes," he answered honestly.

"Well, what are they doing?" she asked more abruptly than she had intended.

"Making chocolate chip cookies."

We all seek to be understood, like the eighteen-month-old and the new bride, but often our inner yearnings to be understood go unfulfilled. Ralph Waldo Emerson said, "It is a luxury to be understood."[40] The scriptures echo the phrase, "They understood not," fourteen times.

It takes sensitivity to understand another's needs. However, there is also a burden on persons wanting to be understood. The new bride is a case in point. She could have prevented feeling misunderstood. When her husband was piling ingredients in the shopping cart, she could have opened a dialogue:

She: Oh, are we going to make chocolate chips cookies?

He: Yes. It's my family's tradition.

She: My family eats pumpkin pie on Christmas Eve.

He: Great. I saw pumpkin pies in the bakery aisle, or do you want to make it from scratch?

Problem solved. Neither feels misunderstood, and more importantly, a healthy pattern of communication is established on day one of their marriage.

When that degree of intimacy cannot or has not been established, it takes the Spirit's help. This principle was illustrated recently when a stake presidency decided to help a local food bank. They planned for members of the stake to go to the food bank, sort food, make deliveries, and do whatever else was needed. E-mails and phone calls went back and forth between a member of the stake presidency and the director of the food bank.

At some point the counselor felt he was much more enthusiastic about the project than was the director of the food bank. The counselor asked if there was a concern with the planned project. (*After all*, he thought, *if you are giving service it might as well be service that is needed and appreciated*.) The openness of the question allowed the director to feel understood. He replied, "With the economy down, demand is up; all we really need is food." If the stake president's counselor had not been sensitive and willing to address the issue, the food bank would have had volunteers forced upon them when all they really needed was food.

Human needs can go unfulfilled if we don't listen to verbal cues and if we don't listen to the Spirit about what others want. We assume people need and will appreciate what we want to give them, and most do. But

---

40 "Quotes," Writers Mugs, http://www.writersmugs.com/quotes.php?day=246.

we can elevate our giving when we seek to understand them, and we should be willing to help others understand us and not expect them to read our minds.

In every religion there is some form of the golden rule: treat others as you would like them to treat you. The negative version has been called the silver rule: don't treat others in ways you would not like to be treated. Whether it's chocolate chip cookies or pumpkin pie, both the gold and silver rules are about understanding, and we can all improve in understanding others better and in helping others to understand us. No matter our best efforts, however, misunderstandings will occur.

When you feel misunderstood, you're in company with Jesus Christ, for even He desired to be understood and wasn't. On the night before He was crucified, He told His Apostles, "My soul is exceeding sorrowful, even unto death." He asked them to stay and watch Him. When He returned, He found them sleeping and begged, "What, could ye not watch with me one hour?" Three times He found them sleeping (see Matthew 26:36–45). In later years, no doubt, the three Apostles relived this experience, wishing they had been more sensitive to His needs, His pain, on that most significant night in the history of the world.

What every living person has in common is the need, the yearning, to be understood. This great gift we can all become better at giving. This ability is a gift of the Spirit and can be obtained the same way other spiritual gifts are obtained. Some receive this gift at birth; others can receive it through prayer as King Solomon did.

The Lord appeared to Solomon in a dream and said, "Ask what I shall give thee." And Solomon answered, "I am but a little child: I know not how to go out or come in. And thy servant is in the midst of thy people. . . . Give therefore thy servant an understanding heart" (1 Kings 3:5–9).

Heavenly Father provides for our wants and needs. If we pray for the gift of wisdom, we can receive an understanding heart and bless others, who, like us, yearn to be understood.

Chapter 35

SUPERHEROES SAVING A SOCIETY IN PERIL

FICTIONAL SUPERHEROES LIKE SUPERMAN AND Batman are motivated to action when the public is in peril. Their goal—to rid the world of crime and corruption.

Mr. Incredible and his wife, Elastigirl, also use their superpowers to rid the world of corruption and crime, but their first goal is to save their family. (If you're not familiar with Mr. Incredible and Elastigirl, they star in the 2004 Disney/Pixar animated movie *The Incredibles*. When they aren't in superhero mode they are Bob and Helen Parr, parents of Violet, Dash, and Jack-Jack.)

Superheroes exist in nonfiction too. We read about some of them in scripture. From the time of Adam and Eve, amazing men and women have worked to save families and preserve freedoms.

One such man was Captain Moroni, who took command of the Nephite armies when he was twenty-five. Helaman described him, saying, "I say unto you, if all men had been, and were, and ever would be, like unto Moroni, behold, the very powers of hell would have been shaken forever" (Alma 48:17).

Captain Moroni gained this reputation by defending the cause of Christians against the very wicked Amalickiah, king of the Lamanites, who wasn't even a Lamanite. Amalickiah used deceit, flattery, poison, and murder in his attempts to destroy the government and the Church of Christ. "And there were many in the church who believed in the flattering words of Amalickiah, therefore they dissented even from the church" (Alma 46:7).

Captain Moroni, in righteous anger, tore off a piece of his coat and wrote on it: "In memory of our God, our religion, and freedom, and our peace, our wives, and our children" (Alma 46:12). He fastened it on the end of a pole and called his flag the title of liberty. Then "he bowed himself to the earth, and he prayed mightily unto his God for the blessings of liberty to rest upon his brethren, so long as there should a band of Christians remain to possess the land" (Alma 46:13).

Then he traveled throughout the land waving the title of liberty and saying in a loud voice, "Behold, whosoever will maintain this title upon the land, let them come forth in the strength of the Lord. . . . When Moroni had proclaimed these words, behold, the people came running together with their armor girded about their loins" (Alma 46:20–21).

Captain Moroni defined what is worth defending—God, religion, freedom, peace, and family. His efforts, combined with others who were likewise motivated to defend these values, defeated evil and saved families and freedoms.

Another Book of Mormon superhero is the great Nephite general, prophet, and historian Mormon, for whom the Book of Mormon is named. He took command of the Nephite armies about 450 years after Captain Moroni. Like Moroni, he tried to motivate his people to fight against tyranny and protect families: "And it came to pass that I did speak unto my people, and did urge them with great energy, that they would stand boldly before the Lamanites and fight for their wives, and their children, and their houses, and their homes" (Mormon 2:23).

Mormon's words were somewhat motivating, but the Nephites had become as wicked as the Lamanites. Mormon summed up their situation: "The strength of the Lord was not with us; yea, we were left to ourselves, that the Spirit of the Lord did not abide in us; therefore we had become weak like unto our brethren [the Lamanites]" (Mormon 2:26). There was no longer a band of Christians to defend their values.

Today we find ourselves in a similarly perilous condition where wickedness is drawing people away from truth. The Lord warned: "Because of the hardness of the hearts of the people . . . except they repent I will take away my word from them, and I will withdraw my Spirit from them, and I will suffer them no longer, and I will turn the hearts of their brethren against them" (Helaman 13:8).

Today President Monson and his counselors figuratively wave the title of liberty—"The Family: A Proclamation to the World." We can only imagine the mighty prayers they say in our behalf. With the Apostles, the First Presidency leads out in defending freedom and family. They are our superheroes, and at each general conference they implore us to cling to God, our religion, freedom, peace, and family.

There are other superheroes among us, but they are walking around as unnoticed as Clark Kent, Bruce Wayne, and Bob and Helen Parr. These superheroes are ordinary men and women who have taken upon themselves the responsibilities of father, mother, grandma, grandpa, aunt, and uncle. They seek the Spirit of the Lord in strength and integrity. Following the prophet, they guide, direct, and protect their families from the enemy of happiness.

Some of these parent-superheroes have created family mottos as one means of achieving family solidarity.

My daughter Michelle wrote,

> When our bishop in California was about to be released after five years of service, he planned a special hike for the families in our ward. He challenged each family in the ward to make a banner to take on the hike, patterned after Captain Moroni's title of liberty that we read about in the Book of Mormon. As our family started to make our own title of liberty, we decided to choose one word for each letter in our last name, Worley. For W, we chose the word *worthy*. For O, we chose *obedient*. R was *righteous*. L was *loving*. E was *eternal*, but we got stuck on Y. After joking around with Y words that made no sense, someone suggested the word *YES*. And so our family title of liberty became our family cheer, and after family prayer each day we put our hands in a circle and say: "Worthy. Obedient. Righteous. Loving. Eternal. YES!"

The Giles family has a family oath: "I am a child of God. I know Heavenly Father has a plan for me, that the Savior lives and will come again. I stand in holy places. I pray always. I study the scriptures daily. I serve and love my family. I remain clean and active as I keep my covenants and honor my father and mother. I am part of an eternal family. I am loved, and I am a Giles." They repeat their family oath after every family prayer, morning and night. It's a tradition to say it twice with a "Go, Giles!" each time. They also created a motto that spells Giles: God-Fearing Inspired Leaders Exemplifying the Savior.

Cynthia's father and mother also had a motto spelling their last name, Budge: Best United Determined Generation Ever. (When Cynthia gave her permission to use these, she said, "You are welcome to use our names, including my mother and father. It seems that it will in some way honor them.")

The Wyatt family's motto, using the letters in their name, is "When You Are Tested, Triumph!" Their story of tests and triumphs can be seen at http://www.youtube.com/watch?v=zgXgWJL927Q.

Because Richard and I have eight children, our motto is "Stren8th." We also had a family meeting when our oldest was about fifteen in which we chose seven family values, one for each letter in Linford. We had nominations for each word and then voted. We ended up with: Loving, Industrious, Nice, Fun, Obedient, Respectful, Diligent.

History will record how we followed the prophets and came forth in the strength of the Lord to save our freedoms and families. As we do, we will defeat evil as superheroes do.

Chapter 36

FATHER MATTERS

WONDERING WHY A CHAPTER ABOUT fathers is in a book that will be read mostly by women? One reason is that "according to the U.S. Census Bureau, 24 million children in America, one out of three, live in biological father-absent homes. Consequently, there is a 'father factor' in nearly all of the social issues facing America today."[41] The homepage of the National Fatherhood Initiative states, "Fatherlessness is America's most pressing social issue."[42] The statistics below show how a father is singularly and critically important to each child and to the nation as a whole. This is not to say that mothers aren't critically important, but mothers tend to be more stable, more attentive, more likely to stick it out through hard times. Statistics bear this out:

"Children in father-absent homes are almost four times more likely to be poor. In 2011, 12 percent of children in married-couple families were living in poverty, compared to 44 percent of children in mother-only families."[43]

"Even after controlling for income, youths in father-absent households still had significantly higher odds of incarceration than those in mother-father families. Youths who never had a father in the household experienced the highest odds."[44]

---

41 "The Father Factor," National Fatherhood Initiative, http://www.fatherhood.org/media/consequences-of-father-absence-statistics.

42 National Fatherhood Initiative, http://www.fatherhood.org.

43 U.S. Census Bureau, *Children's Living Arrangements and Characteristics: March 2011.*

44 Cynthia C. Harper and Sara S. McLanahan, "Father Absence and Youth Incarceration," *Journal of Research on Adolescence*, Vol. 14 (September 2004): 369–97.

"Being raised by a single mother raises the risk of teen pregnancy, marrying with less than a high school degree, and forming a marriage where both partners have less than a high school degree."[45]

"Even after controlling for community context, there is significantly more drug use among children who do not live with their mother and father."[46]

The National Longitudinal Survey of Youth found that obese children are more likely to live in father-absent homes than are non-obese children.[47]

There are pages and pages of statistics shouting the same conclusion: fathers matter! Church leaders have been addressing this fact for decades. Fathers matter so much that the severe warning words used by Jesus Christ to his chief Apostle—"Simon, Simon, behold, Satan hath desired to have you" (Luke 22:31)—were used by a living Apostle to warn young men, fathers, and grandfathers.[48]

Satan is leading a raging battle for the souls of fathers. He preys on all boys and men. It is all-out war. He is organized, focused, and aggressive. How better could he accomplish his goal of destroying families than by diminishing, diluting, and eliminating the role of father? How is he accomplishing this? What are his tools and tactics?

Some men he distracts from home and family with career, money, cars, sports, and other hobbies. He gets some with vanity and pride by telling them rules don't apply to them. He gets some with adultery, some with substance abuse, some with anger and physical abuse. Any boy, man, or father Satan doesn't get by those means, he tries to get with lust and pornography. Never in the history of the world have Satan's temptations besieged boys and men with more intensity.

A man who falls victim to any of these behaviors or addictions cannot fully function as the father he has the potential to be, and his children, to say nothing of his wife, suffer. To the contrary, there are men who defy Satan, who honor and stay true to their wives, who

---

45 Jay D. Teachman, "The Childhood Living Arrangements of Children and the Characteristics of Their Marriages," *Journal of Family Issues*, vol. 25 [January 2004]: 86–111.

46 John P. Hoffmann, "The Community Context of Family Structure and Adolescent Drug Use," *Journal of Marriage and Family*, vol. 64, no. 2, May 2002.

47 See "The Father Factor," National Fatherhood Initiative, http://www.fatherhood.org/media/consequences-of-father-absence-statistics.

48 See Robert D. Hales, "Stand Strong in Holy Places," Ensign, May 2013, 48.

are present in the home and involved in their children's lives. Is there anything better than a man of compassion and empathy who provides a soft landing for his wife and children when hard times come? Is there anything better than a man who works hard to provide for his family as God commanded Adam: "By the sweat of thy face shalt thou eat bread" (Moses 4:25)? Is there anything better than a home in which, because of a father's righteous leadership, the Spirit of the Lord is no stranger?

Father, as outlined in "The Family: A Proclamation to the World," is a sacred title. The proclamation declares that a *father* is to preside in his home, to provide his family with the necessities of life, and to protect them in love and righteousness. Preside, provide, and protect—three powerful principles of manhood and fatherhood. Lofty and elevating in principle but not always easy to achieve in actual practice because being a father is demanding. Fathers first need to be *men*, as Lehi admonished: "Arise from the dust, my sons, and be men" (2 Nephi 1:21). The Apostle Paul explained, "My brethren, be strong in the Lord, and in the power of his might. Put on the whole armour of God, that ye may be able to stand against the wiles of the devil" (Ephesians 6:10–11).

There are men, there are fathers, and there are daddies, of which we have sweet example. When Jesus was in the bitter process of Atonement, "He went forward a little, and fell on the ground, and . . . said, Abba, Father, all things are possible unto thee; take away this cup from me: nevertheless not what I will, but what thou wilt" (Mark 14:35–36).

"Abba, Father" sounds like "Please, Father," or "Dear Father," but it actually has a more important meaning. "To miss the significance of the word *Abba* . . . is to miss the true relationship that existed between Jesus and his Father. The word *Abba* is an Aramaic word meaning 'Papa' or 'Daddy.' It is a form of address signifying the close, intimate, loving, and special bond that develops between some fathers and their children."[49] This loving bond fathers and sons can have fosters happy relationships with the girls and women in their lives.

Ungratefully, some children are more than willing to point out deficiencies in their fathers, when the truth is, if you have a *father,* one who deserves that title, you are one of the privileged. More exceptionally, if you have a father who is also a *daddy,* heaven indeed has smiled on you. Your responsibilities to "Go, and do thou likewise" (Luke 10:37)

---

49 Andrew C. Skinner, *Gethsemane*, Salt Lake City: Deseret Book Company, 2002, 60.

are great—and not only "likewise" but improving on the previous generation.

So why a chapter on fathers in a book for women? Because the important role of father can be greatly aided or undermined by women. God intends for man and woman to be in this together, to be companions. After creating Adam, God said, "It is not good that the man should be alone" (Abraham 5:14). A beautiful union was established. Adam and Eve were created to satisfy each other's needs so neither was alone or lonely. In defining the roles of the man and woman He had just created, God told Adam that Eve was to be a "help meet."

It is not "helpmate," as some have read the words, but two words, "help" and "meet," with meanings and overtones of considerable interest that define Adam and Eve's relationship. Synonyms in various dictionaries include complete, unite, connect, correct, proper, fitting, and equal. The New International Translation reads "a suitable helper." Consider: Eve was given to Adam to complete him. Eve was given to Adam as his equal. Eve was given to Adam to unite them. Eve was given to Adam as a proper, fitting, and correct companion.

In the proclamation, the role of woman and mother is further defined in the word *nurture*, which means to cherish, encourage, enjoy, and support, but it also implies companionship, helpfulness, and awareness and attention to needs and wants. The world may scoff at the seeming simplicity of God's plan, but women who follow this pattern of righteous companionship, of lovingly and willingly helping, and of nurturing husband and children, are doing God's work. When you make father matter, you are doing God's glorious work, for which no calling, cause, or creative desire can compensate.

Chapter 37

THE TRUTH ABOUT UNCONDITIONAL LOVE

As TINA AND KATHY WERE enjoying their biannual lunch date, Tina confided in Kathy that her husband no longer believed in God and was doing things he shouldn't do. Kathy shook her head in disbelief. Tina dabbed at her eyes, brightened a little, and said, "But the solution is to love him unconditionally, right?"

"We don't believe in unconditional love," said Kathy.

"We don't?" Tina asked incredulously.

"We don't," Kathy affirmed. "I'll e-mail you a talk. I believed in unconditional love too, until I read this article."[50]

A few hours later, Tina's reply came. "It's so obvious the difference between divine and unconditional love. Funny the notion of unconditional love is so widespread that everyone just assumes it's true."

That's how Satan works. He takes a principle of the gospel and distorts it. The Apostle Paul warned, "Beware lest any man spoil you through philosophy and vain deceit, after the tradition of men, after the rudiments of the world, and not after Christ" (Colossians 2:8).

Our Father in Heaven and Jesus Christ love inclusively, eternally, and exponentially but not unconditionally because unconditional means *without limits*. If Heavenly Father and Jesus loved and rewarded everyone equally no matter what they did, there would be no reason for heaven or hell. They would require nothing, expect nothing, and judgment would be an empty concept. But the scriptures are clear. Each of us is accountable for how we conduct our lives: "And I saw the dead, small and great, stand before God; and the books were opened: and another book was opened, which is the book of life: and the dead were judged out of

---

50 See Elder Russell M. Nelson, "Divine Love," *Ensign*, Feb. 2003, 20.

those things which were written in the books, according to their works"
(Revelation 20:12).

God told Moses, "For behold, this is my work and my glory—to
bring to pass the immortality and eternal life of man" (Moses 1:39). God
explained to Abraham how immortality and eternal life are achieved.
"We will prove them herewith, to see if they will do all things whatsoever
the Lord their God shall command them" (Abraham 3:25).

We are here on earth to be proved and improved. One of the greatest lessons we learn in this improving process is what happens when we
sin. Heavenly Father doesn't say, "Oh, that's O.K. Just try harder next
time." No. The godly way is to impose a punishment so we learn by
suffering the consequence of our disobedience. The two most common
punishments are 1) blessings are withheld and 2) the Spirit of the Lord
withdraws.

Blessings withheld: You accept and understand that if you keep a
commandment you receive a blessing. One example: "Bring ye all the
tithes into the storehouse . . . and prove me now herewith, saith the
Lord . . . *if* I will not open you the windows of heaven, and pour you out
a blessing, that there shall not be room enough to receive it" (Malachi
3:10). Paying tithing = blessings received. Withholding tithing = blessings
withheld. There are hundreds of conditional promises in scripture, such
as, if you do *this*, then you will receive this blessing, but if you don't do
this, the blessing will be withheld.

2. Spirit withdrawn: A revelation given to Martin Harris through
the Prophet Joseph Smith gives an illustration of having the Spirit taken
away, which the Lord actually said is a "least degree" of punishment.
The Lord said: "I command you again to repent . . . lest you suffer these
punishments of which I have spoken, of which in the smallest, yea, even
in the least degree you have tasted at the time I withdrew my Spirit"
(D&C 19:20). Even though the Lord said it is a small punishment,
losing the Spirit is terrible. When the Spirit departs, it is like turning off
the lights or, using Isaiah's image, "We grope for the wall like the blind,
and we grope as if we had no eyes: we stumble at noonday as in the
night" (Isaiah 59:10). When the Spirit withdraws, our spiritual senses are
dimmed and our defenses against temptation are lessened.

Conditions to being loved by God as fully and completely as He
wants to love us is stated negatively: "*If* you keep not my commandments,

[*then*] the love of the Father shall not continue with you" (D&C 95:12); and positively: The Lord "loveth those who will have him to be their God" (1 Nephi 17:14). The Lord states His conditional love emphatically: "I, the Lord, am bound when ye do what I say; but when ye do not what I say, ye have no promise" (D&C 82:10).

The magnitude of God's love is beyond mortal understanding. He rejoices over the lost sheep that is found and weeps over wandering and rebellious sheep. Enoch saw God weep and asked, "How is it that thou canst weep, seeing thou art holy, and from all eternity to all eternity?" (Moses 7:29). The Lord answered simply, "They are the workmanship of mine own hands, and I gave unto them their knowledge . . . agency . . . and . . . commandment[s] that they should choose me, their Father; but behold, they are without affection. . . . Satan shall be their father, and misery shall be their doom; and the whole heavens shall weep over them, even all the workmanship of mine hands; wherefore should not the heavens weep, seeing these shall suffer?" (Moses 7:32–37).

God doesn't want us to suffer the consequences of disobeying Him. He weeps when we choose evil but can't force us to love Him because love is measured in obedience, service, and loyalty. He never compels His children to love Him because love must be given freely, willingly, and without reservation; yet the door to God's divine, limitless love is always available.

The Savior said, "I stand at the door, and knock: if any man hear my voice, and open the door, I will come in to him, and will sup with him, and he with me" (Revelation 3:20). This is His invitation.

Lyman Wight was a man for whom the heavens wept. The Lord said to him through the Prophet Joseph Smith, "I say unto you that it is my will that my servant Lyman Wight should continue in preaching for Zion, in the spirit of meekness, confessing me before the world; and I will bear him up as on eagles' wings; and he shall beget glory and honor to himself and unto my name" (D&C 124:18). Lyman did not continue in the spirit of meekness and lost claim to the promised blessings.

The importance of understanding God's divine, limitless, and unfathomable love is, as Jesus Christ said, "that they might know thee the only true God, and Jesus Christ, whom thou hast sent" (John 17:3). The better we know His ways, the more He reveals to us. The Prophet Joseph Smith taught, "When we understand the character of God, and know how to come to Him, he begins to unfold the heavens to us, and to tell us all about it. When we are ready to come to him, he is ready to come to us" (Joseph Smith, B. H. Roberts, *History of the Church,* Salt Lake City: Deseret Book Company, 1912, 6:308).

In a subsequent phone conversation, Tina thanked Kathy for teaching her about divine love. She said understanding true doctrine gave her the ability to love her husband but not stand idly by, thinking she had to accept his new lifestyle without setting any conditions on his behavior. She expressed faith that her husband would in time repent and again be one in whom the Lord would "delight to bless with the greatest of all blessings" (D&C 41:1).

Chapter 38

NAUVOO REMEMBERED REALISTICALLY

IT HAS BEEN OVER 167 years since the Mormon pioneers entered the valley of the Great Salt Lake. With the passage of time, it is easy for us to romanticize pioneer life. A brief sampling of health and travel in old Nauvoo, however, reminds us of what daily life was like for them.

Twelve thousand or so members of the Church were forced from Missouri because of mob violence, culminating in Governor Boggs's extermination order. Mormons were to be treated as enemies and either exterminated or driven from the state. It was winter when these desperate refugees arrived in what would become Nauvoo, Illinois, but which at the time was not much more than a swampy outpost called Commerce.

The spongy soil was ideal for the breeding of malaria-carrying mosquitoes, and the weary exiles living in wagons, tents, or on the ground were bait. "The task of building homes was soon exchanged for one of digging graves and caring for the sick. . . . Soon so many entire families were down with the fever that at times there weren't enough healthy people left to care for the sick or even to bury the dead. . . . Sidney Rigdon preached a mass funeral sermon for all the dead."[51] Death visited most every home. In the approximately seven years that Nauvoo was the headquarters of The Church of Jesus Christ of Latter-day Saints, "more than 2,000 people are believed to have died in Nauvoo between 1839 and 1846.[52]

51 George W. Givens, *In Old Nauvoo*, Salt Lake City: Deseret Book Company, 1990, 1–2.
52 "Nauvoo Burial Ground, Nauvoo, Illinois, USA," Mormon Historic Sites Foundation, http://mormonhistoricsites.org/nauvoo-burial-ground.

Though many remedies were tried to treat different illnesses, they were mostly primitive and unscientific. "Scholars seriously believe that doctors were responsible for more deaths than for cures."[53]

The remedies of bloodletting and purging were still being used, as were leeches. One woman, encouraging the use of leeches, wrote to friends, "If you have been with persons who were foolish enough to feel any disgust at leeches, do not be infected by this folly. . . . They are perfectly clean though slippery to the touch."[54] She instructed her friends to "take a piece of blotting-paper and cut small holes in it where you wish them to bite. . . . When they are filled, they will let go their hold."[55]

Bitters, the medicinal name for alcohol and laudanum—a mixture of opium dissolved in alcohol—were commonly used to make the patient more comfortable. Both drugs dulled pain but didn't heal anything. Chimney soot mixed with boiling water and taken three times a day was believed to be a cure for ague and fever. Quinine—a bitter-tasting drug made from the South American cinchona bark—did reduce fever, but the supply was often contaminated and was extremely expensive. A single ounce could cost "as much as a good cow."[56] Death also came from drowning, farm and building accidents, freezing on the open prairie, and travel.

It is 1,245 miles from Nauvoo to Salt Lake City and can be driven in less than twenty hours. The first wagon train took more than seventeen months to travel that route because it included wintering on the west side of the Missouri River. For companies who did not have the layover in Winter Quarters, the 1,245 miles could be traveled in about 111 days.

Most travel was done of necessity, not for pleasure. During rainy weather, bridges washed away and mud made the roads nearly impassable. In 1841, one traveler going to Nauvoo for general conference wrote, "About sunrise it began to rain as we were passing through Carthage. This place is 18 miles from Nauvoo. . . . It rained all day, and we did not get to Nauvoo until 10 o'clock at night."[57] Eighteen hours to go eighteen miles is one mile per hour.

---

53 *In Old Nauvoo*, 117.
54 Ibid., 121.
55 Ibid.
56 Ibid., 116.
57 Ibid., 45.

Travel by stagecoach was also an option, although expensive—at least fifteen times more expensive than bus travel today. Rutted roads made the trip very uncomfortable. Passengers were jostled back and forth, up, down, and sideways. When a coach was ascending a long hill, male passengers had to get out and walk or sometimes push. Passengers would also have to lean left or right as directed by the driver to prevent upsets, which today we would call rollovers.

Upsets were common and caused many injuries and deaths. The safest seats were those in the middle because, as the coach jolted and rocked, the people on the outsides were like pillows for those in the middle. Also, if the coach overturned, those on the outside were like airbags for those in the middle.

The mighty Mississippi could be a faster mode of travel, but it could also be too shallow or too foggy, and there were rapids to navigate, among other risks. "At all times of the year and on all parts of the river were obstructions that made travel hazardous at best and fatal at worst."[58] Besides the risks of running aground, fog, and rapids, river trees could snag and pierce a ship's hull. And then there were boilers. In eighteen months, mid-1841 to the end of 1842, sixty-nine boats were lost—most when the high-pressure boilers that powered the steamboats exploded.

Riding a horse was the most dependable and common means of travel, but many didn't have a horse, let alone a *good* horse. So as it is oftentimes today, a person's feet were the safest and cheapest mode of travel. But unlike today, "individuals on the Illinois frontier usually gave little thought to a walking journey of ten or twenty miles or even more."[59]

Our nostalgia for the good old days, although sometimes not realistic, is understandable. Even while they were being expelled, some who had lived there shared similar sentiments. Wilford Woodruff, who became the fourth President of the Church, shared his emotions as he looked at Nauvoo for the last time: "I was in Nauvoo on the 26th of May, 1846, for the last time, and left the city of the Saints feeling that most likely I was taking a final farewell of Nauvoo for this life. I looked upon the temple and city as they receded from view and asked the Lord to remember the sacrifices of His Saints."[60] His prayer is fulfilled as we

---

58 Ibid., 34.
59 Ibid., 48.
60 Matthias F. Cowley, *Wilford Woodruff, His Life and Labors*, Salt Lake City: Deseret Book Company, 1909, 248.

remember the pioneers in the hardships and devotions. Blessed, honored pioneers.

Chapter 39

HAPPINESS AND THE BOOK OF MORMON

AN EIGHT-YEAR-OLD BOY, TOM, RAN away from home because of severe abuse. He ended up near a beach in Southern California. Tom gave his permission to use his story: "Please feel free to use it. I will always fondly remember and love Huntington Beach. I spent most of my time around the pier (which has since burned down and been rebuilt). I think the Jack-In-The-Box fast food restaurant is still there. I can see it all very clearly in my mind's eye—of course, I see it all as it was forty-eight years ago."

This began a pattern for the next eight years of Tom's life. He was in and out of foster care, in and out of juvenile detention, and in between, he lived on the beach and attended school sporadically. When he was sixteen, he was back on the beach during the winter. Sometimes when it was extra cold, he would go into the Jack In The Box to get warm because the people there did not turn him away and sometimes would give him something to eat.

One day the owner came up to Tom and said, "Would you like a job?"

"What kind of a job?" Tom asked.

"It would be reading to my eight-year-old son, who is hydrocephalic. He's very ill and can't go to school."

"I guess so," Tom agreed. That started a friendship between a dying eight-year-old and a homeless sixteen-year-old.

At first Tom read Dr. Seuss, fairy tales, and children's classics—books he had never read before. After several months, he had read all the children's books in the family library. "So what shall I read now?" Tom asked.

The eight-year-old said, "Let's get to the good stuff. See that blue book over there on the shelf?" That blue book was the Book of Mormon.

The owner of the Jack In The Box was the local LDS bishop. Tom learned the gospel by reading the Book of Mormon and hearing the doctrine from an eight-year-old. Tom joined the Church, went on a mission, got married in the temple, and has been a bishop and a mission president. The Book of Mormon changes lives.

Robert Mack Gray Jr. wrote a book about his addiction experiences, *The Unseen Enemy*, which is used in some addiction-recovery programs. (The book is online at http://mentalhealthlibrary.info/library/add/ addlds/addldsauthor/links/addldsstories/enemy/partone.htm.) When he was thirteen, Bob began to drink. He shared the depths of his degradation in this statement: "Hi, my name is Bob. I'm an alcoholic in the first degree, drug addict in the second. I am also the proud owner of an assortment of the most filthy thoughts imaginable."[61] He lived like that for seventeen years. He recalls, "I was in complete bondage to alcohol and drugs. . . . Nothing short of a real live miracle was going to stop me from drinking and using drugs."[62]

That miracle occurred the last time Bob stayed in a detox center:

> I don't know how many miles I paced back and forth that night, but being totally exhausted and in the greatest anguish, I went to my room to lie down. There on the table by the bed was something that had been following me my whole life: a Book of Mormon. I looked away. The sight of it scorched me. You see, I was raised a Mormon and quit going to church as soon as my parents got tired of making me go, but there were things I was taught as a little boy that were written in my heart.
>
> I made a choice that day that saved my life. . . . Not having much hope at all, I read a few pages and did something that had become strange to me—I said a prayer. This prayer was different from all the rest of my prayers. It came from my heart. I had finally reached the point where I humbled myself enough to ask for some big-time help. I was too dazed to realize it at the time, but it really was the best day of my life.

While in detox, Bob turned thirty. When it came time to leave, he was afraid of himself and the choices he might make. He didn't know what to do or where to go. These are his words:

---

61 *The Unseen Enemy*, 5.
62 Ibid., 9, 13.

Hopelessness began to engulf me, [and] in the midst of my awful contemplations a blue Buick pulled up right in front of me. . . . I recognized the car. It was my mom. She always had hope for me. . . . [Isn't that wonderful! His mother always had hope, and he knew it.] At home, I walked into my old room. It was cool, familiar, and clean. . . . Then I saw it lying on the table by my bed—the Book of Mormon. I picked the book up and started reading like a madman. . . . I stopped reading long enough to go to AA that night. When I came home, I commenced reading again. The wall that had been cutting me off had finally broken. I felt an unquenchable thirst for what I was reading. A strange sense of peace came over me, and I felt that maybe there was a way out of this mess.

Bob kept reading the Book of Mormon, praying, and attending AA. Weeks turned into months, and he was still sober. He has been clean and sober for over fourteen years. The Book of Mormon changes lives.

How does the Book of Mormon change lives? It teaches about Heavenly Father's great plan of happiness—where we came from, why we're here on earth, and what happens after we die. If you look up the word *plan* in scripture, you'll find it's used forty-seven times: zero times in the Bible, three times in the Doctrine and Covenants, once in the Pearl of Great Price, and forty-three times in the Book of Mormon! If you look up how many times the word *happiness* occurs in scripture, you'll discover that it's found thirty-two times: zero times in the Bible, one time in the Doctrine and Covenants, one time in the Pearl of Great Price, and thirty times in the Book of Mormon! So the question "Where do you find happiness?" is literally answered: "In the Book of Mormon."

Chapter 40

I Trust Him

A LETTER READ TO ORDINANCE workers in the Salt Lake Temple in January 2012 said that those who didn't live in the geographic boundaries of the Salt Lake Temple district would be released effective June 1. A woman affected by the change sent an e-mail to her temple friends.

"As I leave the Salt Lake Temple in June after serving twenty years—due to living outside the temple district—I shall remember all of you with such love in my heart. It breaks my heart to have to go. I wonder why Heavenly Father feels it is so important to serve in the district you live in. I don't know the answer, but I trust Him."

"I trust in Him" is a statement of belief and faith. "I trust in Him" is a declaration of reliance upon God and a surrendering of one's will to Him.

A thirty-five-year-old husband and father of five started having a tremor in his right hand. Then he began stumbling while dribbling on the basketball court. A few months later, he fell while running. He seemed to become fatigued with very little exertion. His wife persuaded him to see a doctor, where he received a most unwelcome diagnosis—Parkinson's, a progressive, degenerative disease. How does he feel about such devastating news? Horrible! He knows life is hard enough without adding the complication of a degenerative disease. Still, he said, "I don't know why this is happening to me, but I trust Heavenly Father does."

When Hezekiah, the king of Judah, realized that Sennacherib, king of Assyria, was encamped in Judah with plans to fight against Jerusalem, Hezekiah's actions could be called the definition of trust:

He consulted with his princes and mighty men.

His princes, mighty men, and people worked together to "stop the waters of the fountains which were without the city" so that the Assyrians would have no water.

They "built up all the wall that was broken" and raised up the towers.

They "made darts and shields in abundance."

He organized them and "set captains of war over the people."

He gathered the captains together and "spake comfortably to them" saying: "Be strong and courageous, be not afraid nor dismayed for the king of Assyria, nor for all the multitude that is with him: for there be more with us than with him: With him is an arm of flesh; but with us is the Lord our God to help us, and to fight our battles" (2 Chronicles 32:7–8).

When Sennacherib's men began a campaign to discredit Hezekiah and frighten the people by telling the people that they were going to die by famine and thirst and that their God couldn't save them, King Hezekiah and the prophet Isaiah prayed together (see 2 Chronicles 32:1–21).

When you trust in God, you do all you can and leave the rest to your Father in Heaven. What happened to Hezekiah and his people? "The Lord sent an angel" (2 Chronicles 32:21) to fight their battles. Defeated, Sennacherib returned to Assyria, where his own children killed him. We worship a mighty God, who is worthy of our trust. Twenty-one times in scripture, the Lord commands that we trust Him. King David said, "It is better to trust in the Lord than to put confidence in man" (Psalm 118:8).

Trusting in Heavenly Father is personal and sacred. Your private prayers are known only by Him. The Holy Ghost carries thoughts, solutions, comfort, and love into the confidential chambers of your mind and heart. Your trust in God is your testimony of His omniscience and is evidence that you understand that trust is reciprocal. You desire more than anything else to have Him trust you.

He delights to bless you, and you delight to obey Him. You trust His promises are sure, and He trusts you with personal guidance and testimony. You know "when [you] obtain any blessing from God, it is by obedience to that law upon which it is predicated" (D&C 130:21). So you continue to pay tithing through economic downturns. You keep the Sabbath day holy though temptations constantly beckon. You obey the Ten Commandments even when you stand alone. Through sunshine and storm, your trust stays constant. King David wrote, "Trouble and anguish have taken hold on me: yet thy commandments are my delights" (Psalm 119:143). Attached to His commandments are promises and blessings that He is anxious to shower upon you. He said, "The Lord God of your fathers make you a thousand times so many more as ye are, and bless you, as he hath promised you" (Deuteronomy 1:11).

Alma said, "O, my son Helaman . . . I do know that whosoever shall put their trust in God shall be supported in their trials, and their troubles, and their afflictions" (Alma 36:3). Nephi said, "I know in whom I have trusted . . . He [that] hath heard my cry" (2 Nephi 4:19, 23). King David said, "Blessed are all they that put their trust in him" (Psalm 2:12).

Trust in God is willingness to wait to understand the reasons why you have to leave a calling you have loved for twenty years, why you have a life-threatening or life-altering disease, why your peaceful land is being threatened by invading forces. Life is full of whys: Why did she die? Why was he born blind? Why haven't I married? Why is my child rebellious? Why did I lose my job? Why? Why? Why?

An aspect of trusting in God is patience. The scriptural definition of patience is to "wait upon the Lord." "And I will wait upon the Lord . . . and I will look for him" (2 Nephi 18:17). "Our eyes wait upon the Lord our God, until that he have mercy upon us" (Psalm 123:2). "Blessed are all they that wait for him" (Isaiah 30:18). "But they that wait upon the Lord shall renew their strength; they shall mount up with wings as eagles; they shall run, and not be weary; and they shall walk, and not faint" (Isaiah 40:31).

Although we may ask, "Why this? Why that? Why now? Why me?" Trust is doing all you can do and watching the miracles unfold. At some point you trust enough to say, "Why not me? I trust Him."

Chapter 41

Will Heaven Feel Like Home When You Get There?

ON MAY 31, 2011, PROFESSOR Lynn Williams gave the BYU devotional address. The choir opened by singing "My Little Welsh Home" because Professor Williams is a Welshman. Though he came to the United States in 2000, his Welsh heritage is still very much a part of his identity. Before he came to the United States, he had seen so many American television shows that he thought he understood Americans. He admitted he was wrong. He likened this feeling to thinking we know a lot about heaven because we go to church and talk about it. But, he asked, "Can we be sure that heaven will be a familiar place when we get there? Or will we experience the kind of culture shock I experienced in the United States?"[63]

He grew up in a small Welsh village, joined the Church at fourteen, and at eighteen, was off to London to further his education. His memories of his last Sunday in Wales are vivid. At the end of the meetings, a tenor suddenly stood up and began to sing to him. Professor Williams acknowledged that "anywhere else such an occurrence would probably seem very odd indeed. In those days it wasn't quite so odd in Wales. In fact, the rest of the congregation soon joined the tenor. Sweet nostalgia drips from every phrase and bids all Welshmen to return home to Wales. One of the phrases uses the word *hiraeth*."[64]

Professor Williams explained the word *hiraeth* has no exact equivalent in English. It references the stirring or voice that calls all Welshmen who venture abroad back home to Wales. But longing for home isn't something that just happens to people born in Wales.

---

63 Lynne Williams, "Will Heaven Feel Like Home When We Get There?" BYU Speeches, http://speeches.byu.edu/?act=viewitem&id=1960.
64 Ibid.

I recall reading about a woman who grew up in what she considered the best place under heaven. (I can't recall where it was, so let's say it was Kentucky.) Even when she went away to college, she returned during the summers to feel at home, and thoughts of home kept her going when she was away at school. Then she married and moved where her husband found work.

She tolerated living there for several years, and several children were born into their family, but in her quiet moments she transported herself to her "old Kentucky home." Her husband was not insensitive to the fact that he had taken her away from all that was familiar. For several years, her longing for home hurt his pride that he and their little family weren't enough to help her feel at home.

She knew she needed to stop nostalgia-izing about wanting to live by people who spoke, thought, and acted like she did. She got involved in the ward and served in the parent/teacher association of the elementary school. She made a good effort to acclimatize and immerse herself in the community and did make a "home" for her family. However, as you've heard, "You can take the girl out of Kentucky, but you can't take Kentucky out of the girl."

Then her husband came home with the astonishing news that his company had just purchased a company in Kentucky and that he was the new manager. They were moving to Kentucky! How happy she was to be going home. And I'm sure you know what happened next. No, she didn't miss where they lived; instead, she found that deep inside she still longed for home. After much prayer, fasting, and a priesthood blessing, she realized her homesickness was for her heavenly home.

Professor Williams expressed a similar feeling. He said,

> I like to think that as each of us prepared to leave our premortal estate for our adventure on earth, a tenor came forward and, quickly joined by a heavenly choir, began to sing. . . . I hope that, in our quieter moments, we sense or hear a voice from beyond the veil that calls us home. I hope we occasionally experience *hiraeth*, that yearning to return to our heavenly home, that place where there are no 'strangers or foreigners' and where there is indeed a love that never fails.
>
> The voice we need to listen for is, of course, the voice of the Spirit. As we listen, memories will come flooding

back, and we will want to turn homeward. Each time we heed the Spirit's voice, we move one step closer to home. Remember that it is what we feel more than what we see or hear that remains etched in our memories.[65]

Professor Williams closed his talk, and a lone tenor stood and sang the same refrain Professor Williams had heard that last Sunday in Wales.

Have you felt that nostalgia for heaven and heavenly things? Have you desired with Lehi to behold God's glory and feel His encircling arms around you? (See 2 Nephi 1:15.) Perhaps you've had fragmentary glimpses that somewhat satisfy your homesickness—in your prayers, during the sacrament, in the temple, in nature, at births or deaths, in giving service, when you feel truly understood, when singing or hearing music filled with the Spirit, or when unexpected thoughts come as impressions from the Holy Ghost.

Isaac Watts (1674–1748) expressed this desire of what his heavenly home will feel like: "No more a stranger or a guest, but like a child at home." (These words have been set to music. You can hear the Tabernacle Choir sing "My Shepherd Will Supply My Need" at http://www.youtube.com/watch?v=70kdwGBv8fQ.)

As you savor these experiences, you are being prepared so that when you do get to heaven, you will feel you have come home.

---

65 Ibid.

Chapter 42

WHAT TEN THOUSAND HOURS GUARANTEE

"THAT WHICH WE PERSIST IN doing becomes easier, not that the task itself has become easier, but that our ability to perform it has improved," said Ralph Waldo Emerson. President Heber J. Grant made Emerson's words famous in Latter-day Saint culture by his personal tenacity to difficult tasks: "That which we persist in doing becomes easier for us to do; not that the nature of the thing itself is changed, but that our power to do is increased" (*Conference Report*, April 1901, 63).

President Grant's "persistence in his youth is legendary. . . . He got [good] at marbles. He earned a spot on a baseball team after being called a 'sissy'—and they went on to win the championship. He was told that his writing was like lightning had struck an ink bottle, or like chicken tracks—yet he eventually taught penmanship at the university. Most amazing of all, he was successful in learning to sing when he was tone deaf. His tone deafness was so profound that if his back was to the piano and you hit the highest note and the lowest note, he couldn't tell the difference."[66]

But President Grant was determined to sing in such a way that those who were listening would not wish they were forty miles away. It was reported that he sang one hundred hymns on a trip to Arizona and that to learn to sing "O, My Father," he practiced it five thousand times. Once, when he was eighty, he went on a cruise to Alaska. "He and some of his family were gathered around a piano singing, and someone said, 'President Grant, would you like to sing a solo?' The family's response: 'Oh, no.' President Grant's response: 'Oh, I'd be glad to.' He sang 'The Flag Without a Stain,' and people began to gather even from the lower

---

66 Truman G. Madsen, *Presidents of the Church*, Salt Lake City: Deseret Book, 2004.

decks, listening, incredulous, not because it was so poor, but because it was so strong, and they applauded when he was finished."[67] It's logical. You keep doing something, and you get better at it. But how much better and how soon?

Malcoln Gladwell's book *Outliers* is subtitled, "The Story of Success," and if there is a true secret to success, his idea has merit and credibility. In chapter 2, "The 10,000-Hour Rule," he gives evidence to support his theory that it takes 10,000 hours to get really, really good at something. He uses the examples of the Beatles and Bill Gates.

When the Beatles came to America in 1964, they had been playing together for seven years. John Lennon said of this time, "In Liverpool, we'd only ever done one-hour sessions, and we just used to do our best numbers, the same ones, at every one."[68] Then they got a job playing in Hamburg, Germany. Lennon continued, "In Hamburg, we had to play for eight hours, so we really had to find a new way of playing. . . . We got better and got more confidence. We couldn't help it with all the experience playing all night long."[69] They performed 270 nights in eighteen months, which sounds like a lot, but 270 nights times 8 hours equals only 2,160 hours. The more they played, however, the better they got and the more opportunities to perform came. At the peak of their career, they had spent ten years playing together and had logged in excess of ten thousand hours.

Next, Gladwell presents evidence for his 10,000-hour theory in the life of Bill Gates. In 1968, when Gates was in the seventh grade, his parents sent him to a private school because he complained of being bored in public school. At his new school, they just happened to have a computer—unusual, considering at the time, most *colleges* didn't have computers.

Bill and some friends began to teach themselves how to use this new device, spending all the hours the teachers would allow. Bill remembers that by high school, "it was my obsession. I skipped athletics. I went up there at night. We were programming on weekends. It would be a rare week that we wouldn't get twenty or thirty hours in."[70] Because he got in on the ground floor, he became an expert before others even learned how

---

67 Ibid.
68 Malcolm Gladwell, *Outliers: The Story of Success*, New York: Little, Brown and Company, 2008, 49.
69 Ibid.
70 Ibid., 52.

to program. Consequently, because of his early expertise, more and more opportunities presented themselves. Bill's introduction to computers began when he was twelve, and by the time he dropped out of Harvard when he was about nineteen, he had spent almost eight years doing nothing but programming.

Success comes with a price tag of time, energy, and focus. Whether you sing one hymn five thousand times or play in a band eight hours at a time or sit at a computer all night long, if you do it over and over and over, you get really good. And what is the result? Opportunities come.

The critical part of the 10,000-hour idea is that we all—every one of us—have the same number of hours in every day, and we are going to spend our 10,000 hours doing something. Choice, that blessed gift of agency, allows us to decide how we use our time. No matter how well we manage, mismanage, or waste the time given to us, the results follow. This is not rocket science. If we persist, our power to do increases.

Chapter 43

THE FOREKNOWLEDGE OF GOD

WENDY WALKS MANY MORNINGS FOR exercise and to spend time with her husband, Toney. On Memorial Day, they walked a different route for no particular reason. As they were walking in front of an elementary school, they saw a mother drive up with her little daughter, who looked like she was in kindergarten. The little girl got out of the car, put her backpack on her back, and started to walk toward the school. Wendy and Toney heard the mother wish her child a good day at school. As the mother started to drive away, it dawned on Wendy that it was Memorial Day and school was closed. She ran after the mother, yelling for her to stop. When she stopped, Wendy explained that there was no school, and the little girl returned to the car. The what-ifs are frightening. A little child was protected because of the foreknowledge of God, who guided Wendy and Toney to be at that particular spot at that exact moment.

When I was a student at the University of Utah, I met a friend who had been raised in the Church. We talked many times during our first term because she was taking philosophy and her spiritual foundations were being rattled. One troubling issue we discussed was whether or not God had all knowledge or if He was progressing. Her professor taught that if God knows everything that is going to happen, then humans don't have free will, they are just actors in melodramatic play. The professor taught that God, if there really was such a being, wasn't all-knowing because humans can use their free will in ways that surprise Him.

I knew then as I do now that Heavenly Father knows the end from the beginning. He has a plan for every contingency.

"But if that's true," my friend argued, "then we really don't have free will."

At the time, I didn't know any scriptures to read with her, and the *Encyclopedia of Mormonism* had not been written, but I did know there was a book in my parents' bookcase called *Mormon Doctrine* by Elder Bruce R. McConkie, who was one of the Twelve Apostles. I went home, copied what Elder McConkie said about God's foreknowledge, and gave it to my friend. Basically, Elder McConkie said that the notion that God is still learning and growing in intelligence is completely false. There is nothing He has yet to learn. Earth is not His laboratory, and we are not an experiment. He knows all and has all power.

I told her I believed Heavenly Father knows everything that will happen to us but we don't. He could have dispensed with earth life and just told us what choices we would make. He could have given us a list or showed us a video of the sins we would commit and the command-ments we wouldn't obey. He could have assigned us a kingdom based on His infinite wisdom. I think we would have protested and said, "Oh no. I won't do those things. I'll be faithful under any and all circumstances. Let me go to earth, and I'll prove that I will keep Thy commandments and serve Thee to the end." Thus, earth life is time when we prove our-selves to ourselves.

In that proving process, we are not left on our own. We have the blessing of praying to our Father in Heaven and receiving His divine help. We have the Atonement of Jesus Christ, which allows us to be forgiven when we repent. We have the Holy Ghost to guide us to truth. In these basic ways, our Father's plan of salvation unfolds for each of us. When bad things happen and we humble ourselves before Him, He makes whatever happens bearable and not only bearable but ultimately glorious.

In April 2011, a shed caught on fire. The firefighters had to approach the fire through Jason and Cynthia's yard. Cole, their four-year-old son, watched. As a result of this experience Cole became fascinated with fire-fighters. He wanted to be a firefighter when he grew up and pretended he was a firefighter so much that Cynthia bought him his first fireman's costume in September 2011. His fascination continued. So Cynthia and Jason took Cole to the fire station a couple of times, and the firefighters kindly showed him their equipment.

About midnight on June 24, 2012, Jason noticed the neighbor's house was on fire. Three hook-and-ladder trucks arrived on their street. The fam-ilies in the homes on either side were evacuated. When Cynthia woke up Cole, she dressed him in his fireman's costume. As they were leaving the house, a firefighter saw Cole and said, "Hey, you're a fireman too. Come here, and you can help me hold the hose and squirt water on the fire."

The trauma of seeing the house next door burn down was greatly lessened by previous positive experiences with firefighters. Heavenly Father kindly prepared Cole and his parents for an extremely difficult situation.

One day I felt I had offended a son-in-law—not purposefully but because of my basic insensitivity to others' needs. When I couldn't find him to apologize, I asked where he was and was told he had gone to a relative's house. I asked my daughter Christine to walk with me to the relative's house to apologize. When we got to the relative's house, my son-in-law was not there.

As Christine and I walked out of the house, some crazy mood came over me, and I started skipping and dancing down the street until I saw Selena, who lives next door to my relative, sitting on her front porch talking on her cell phone. I thought she was crying. I chastised myself again for insensitivity to yet another person. In a few days, I learned Selena had just been diagnosed with breast cancer. I put two and two together and assumed that was what she was crying about when I was doing a jig in front of her house. I hoped she would be at church on Sunday so I could apologize.

Richard and I sat in our usual place that next Sunday, and Selena and her children came and sat behind us, something they'd never done before. As soon as the closing amen was said, I stood up, turned around, and hugged her; she started to cry. I told her how sorry I was that she had joined the breast cancer club and that I was so boisterous a few nights before when she was crying on the phone. Then she said, "Oh, Marilynne. I'm not crying because I have breast cancer, I'm crying because of the night you were doing the little jig down my street. You see, I was praying for a sign of some kind that Heavenly Father was aware of my situation and that everything would be okay. I knew how sick you had been when you had breast cancer, and there you were dancing down my street. You were the answer to my prayers."

The foreknowledge of God is assured by scripture: "All things are present before mine eyes" (D&C 38:2). He knows the past, present, and future, "things as they are, and as they were, and as they are to come" (D&C 93:24). Consequently, His foreknowledge includes our thoughts, hopes, fears, desires, vulnerabilities, strengths, and our interconnectedness with every other person. As in the examples of Selena, Cole, and the little girl being dropped off when there was no school, many consecutive steps had to be in place for the desired outcome to be achieved. These are not isolated instances but likely happen every day to anyone who seeks to see God's hand in her life.

His foreknowledge allows His continuous and constant love. You can feel completely safe in His care. A woman experiencing great hardship said, "I don't understand all that God does, but I know whatever He does He does with great love."

Chapter 44

LOVE AND AFFECTION

ABOUT TWENTY YEARS AGO, THE young women of the East Mill Creek 11th Ward offered the men in the ward the opportunity to purchase a singing Valentine for their wives. The young women learned the songs, practiced the actions, and got as good as professionals. They even wrote some of the words. On Valentine's Day, they delivered a corny but cute singing valentine to homes in the ward:

> (To the tune of "You Are My Sunshine")
> You are my sunshine, my only sunshine,
> You're like a special kind of glue
> You are my soul mate, to you I resonate,
> I really love you, yes I do!

> (To the tune of "Daisy, Daisy")
> _____, _____, I have a message for you.
> I'm still crazy all for the love of you.
> Our marriage has been a dandy
> You're sweet as sugar candy.
> You're kind and neat, my heart does beat,
> For you on this Valentine's.

Then the bishopric decided to send a Valentine's Day wish to the widows in the ward via the young women. Their message was to the tune of "Row, Row, Row Your Boat."

> We're here to wish to you a happy Valentine
> From some folks who think that you truly are sublime.
> You are kind and special too, really rather slick,
> This message comes direct to you—from your bishopric!

The young women made a lot of women happy that evening, including themselves. Valentine's Day is only one of every day we should celebrate others and increase our ability to express love and affection.

Natalie went to her granddaughter's preschool program, accidently arriving thirty minutes early. Gradually, the room began to fill, and Natalie began to notice a pattern. The mother would arrive with her preschooler, take the child to his or her teacher, return to the main room, and take a seat. Within a few minutes, the husband would arrive and sit down near his wife.

Natalie watched perhaps twenty couples come together. Some couples acted as if they were divorced, hardly giving each other a brief glance, no polite greeting, smile, or even eye contact. Honestly, most were too busy with their cell phones.

A few wives, however, watched anxiously for their husbands to walk through the door. An especially sweet scene unfolded as one young wife and mother watched the door until her husband came in. She stood up and waved to get his attention. When he got to her, she put the palm of her hand on his chest. Then they smiled at each other, shared a quick kiss, and chatted happily until the program started. This sweet and refreshing display of affection contrasted with the indifference of many of the other couples.

Probably most of the couples at the preschool program love each other, and love is good. But love is not affection.

Affection in marriage makes the love between a man and a woman tender and close. Marital affection shows contentment and security. Affection is mutual, not one-sided. Affection between spouses shows that each understands the other well enough to take a hand, give a little hug or kiss, smile with loving eyes, whisper a kind word, and perceive unspoken needs. Affection is given and received. Affection takes but a moment here and a moment there. Affection passes between a married couple as it were outside of time and space.

The "love" shown between men and women on television and in movies is mostly devoid of affection. This counterfeit love is all about self-gratification rather than mutual satisfaction. In real love, affection is expressed genuinely and is realized in closeness, care, concern; it's consistent and selfless.

Love, shown with appropriate affection, creates the healthiest environment to which children can come. When children are welcomed into such a family, stable and secure relationships grow between parents and children and among siblings. Affection respects and reciprocates. Affection is warm and friendly. Affection is a safety net, an inoculation against divorce. Affection in marriage sweetens life's trials and adversities. In such a home, "there *is* beauty all around" (*Hymns*, no. 294, emphasis added).

John H. McNaughton has added a couple verses to this much-beloved hymn, which bespeaks affection. (I changed his words slightly):

Love becomes a way of life,
when there's love at home;
sweet, consistent end to strife,
when there's love at home.
Glad submission is one's gift,
willingly to love and lift,
healing balm for every rift,
when there's love at home.

Anger cools and pressures cease,
when there's love at home;
Children learn to live in peace,
when there's love at home. . . .
Sharing joy in work or play,
confidence to face the day,
Knowing love will find a way,
when there's love at home.[71]

Most likely, today is not Valentine's Day, but every 365 days can be like a Valentine's Day when there is giving and receiving of both love—the cake—and affection—the frosting.

---

71 "Love at Home," Timeless Truths, http://library.timelesstruths.org/music/Love_at_Home/.

Chapter 45

THE TONE IN THE HOME

A CARTOON SHOWS TWO PARENTS in a car with two teenage boys in the backseat. The father has on a brightly flowered shirt, sunglasses, a couple days' growth of beard, and a very bored expression. The two sons have folded arms over their chests and look grumpy. Mother is wearing a straw hat with a green band and a green shirt. She is reading a magazine as they drive along. She says, "Here is a family doing the same trip that we are, but having fun."

Is this cartoon about family vacations? Superficially, perhaps, but what happens on vacations is a reflection of a family's home life. By the expressions on the faces, we can easily evaluate this family's ability to communicate, interact, and express love. When families that don't know how to get along are confined in close proximity—like in a car or hotel room—frustrations often surface.

Learning to get along as a family is challenging in every stage, from birth to death. Every family has challenges and adversities. Not every moment of family life is peaches and cream, even in the happiest of families, because home is where personalities are refined, needs met, wants tempered, solutions configured, and where kindness is the rule rather than the exception.

It's been said, "If Mama ain't happy, ain't nobody happy." Likewise, "If Papa ain't happy, ain't nobody happy." A happy home rests on the parents' relationship, which is a measure of how they treat each other. The common courtesies of "please" and "thank you" are as vital to a marriage as rain to a thirsty desert. The softness of the voice, the smile on the face, the kindness of the words, the patience in adjusting to the unexpected, and the mercy that comes from forgiveness provide a firm foundation of unity and love.

Every marriage has ups and downs. The secret to experiencing more ups than downs is to keep the marriage in a constant state of repenting, repairing, and rebuilding so that no irritant can fester. Whether your marriage is up, down, or in-between right now, Dr. John Gottman, who studied marriage for forty years, has a suggestion that can improve all marriage relationships.

At the Gottman Institute site is a quiz you can take that will show how well you know your spouse (http://www.gottman.com/how-well-do-you-know-your-partner). Number four reads: "I can tell you some of my partner's life dreams." This is an important theme in Gottman's work. He relates an experience of when one of his books was going to be published by a New York City publisher. He had an appointment with the marketing director to discuss the best way to sell the book. The first words the marketing director said were, "In thirty seconds, what should I do to make my marriage better?"

Dr. Gottman answered something like, "The most important thing you can do in marriage is to know and honor your wife's dreams."

With no warning, the marketing director got up out of his chair and left the room. Dr. Gottman had no idea where he went or if he would be back. It turned out, the man had left the building, walked to the subway, and gone home. When his wife saw him home in the middle of the day, she said, "What are you doing here? Did you get fired?"

"No, he said. "I just have to know what your dreams are."

She looked at him for a long moment and said, "I thought you'd never ask."[72]

Married couples who aren't aware of or don't care about each other's dreams, goals, hopes, and fears, lead parallel lives, each focusing on his or her own needs. However, when husband and wife help fulfill each other's dreams, the synergy of two individuals sitting in the same boat rowing in the same direction creates a culture of unity, trust, and appreciation. Such a marriage is an oasis from the cares of the world.

As spouses learn from each other, taking the best and discarding the rest, a sweet and powerful blending helps them become one. In *The Enchanted April*, Elizabeth Von Armin describes Mr. and Mrs. Wilkins:

"Nobody took any notice of Mrs. Wilkins. She was the kind of person who is not noticed at parties. Her clothes, infested by thrift, made

---

72 "How Can I Improve My Marriage in 30 Seconds?" YouTube, http://www.youtube.com/watch?v=G_Vz_Cbsu3o&feature=c4-overview&list=UUnT1R08f7F HLab3nB4f0AGQ.

her practically invisible; her face was non-arresting; her conversation was reluctant; she was shy."[73]

Mr. Wilkins was a "clean-shaven fine-looking man, who gave a party, merely by coming to it, a great air. Wilkins was very respectable. He was known to be highly thought of by his senior partners. His sister's circle admired him. He pronounced adequately intelligent judgments on art and artists. He was pithy; he was prudent; he never said a word too much, nor . . . did he ever say a word too little."[74]

You could say Mr. and Mrs. Wilkins have serious incompatibility issues. She is thinking of separation and goes on vacation with some other women to consider her options.

At some point she realizes, "I was a stingy beast at home, and used to measure and count. I had a queer obsession about justice. As though justice mattered. As though justice can really be distinguished from vengeance. It's only love that's any good. At home I wouldn't love [my husband] unless he loved me back, exactly as much, absolute fairness. . . . And as he didn't, neither did I, and the *aridity* of that house."[75]

Aridity describes a sterile, dull, dreary, desertlike ecosystem. But aridity, like so many other "issues" in marriage and family life, isn't fatal. Farther into *The Enchanted April*, we read that Mr. Wilkins "was determined to please, and he did please. He was most amiable to his wife—not only in public, which she was used to, but in private, when he certainly wouldn't have been if he hadn't wanted to. He did want to. . . . And the more he treated her as though she were really very nice, the more [she] expanded and became really very nice, and the more he, affected in his turn, became really very nice himself; so that they went round and round, not in a vicious but in a highly virtuous circle."[76]

Mr. Wilkins is an example of a husband who looked for the good in his spouse and looked for what was going right in the marriage rather than what was going wrong. Because his wife felt loved and valued, she reciprocated by loving and valuing him. Feeling loved and valued creates harmony and happiness.

Families who enjoy this tone in the home *like* being together at home or on vacation. They manage the normal ups and downs of family

---

73 Elizabeth Von Arnim, *The Enchanted April*, Seven Treasures Publications, 2009, 6.
74 Ibid., 6–7.
75 Ibid., 83.
76 Ibid., 121.

life without ill temper, sulking, or accusing. His needs are her needs, and her needs are their needs. "Round and round they go, not in a vicious but in a highly virtuous circle."[77] In such a home, the Spirit of the Lord is no stranger.

---

[77] Ibid., 121.

Chapter 46

IS DIVORCE THE ANSWER?

DR. LINDA J. WAITE AT the University of Chicago designed her research to answer the question, "Does divorce typically make adults happier than staying in an unhappy marriage?"[78] You would assume the answer is *yes*. That assumption is called the *divorce assumption*. You may think that people in an unhappy marriage have only two choices—stay married and be miserable or divorce and be happier. Dr. Waite's research team tested that assumption, and the results challenge conventional wisdom. They found no evidence that unhappily married adults who divorced were any happier than those who stayed married.

"Even more dramatically, the researchers also found that two-thirds of unhappily married spouses who stayed married reported that their marriages were happy five years later. In addition, the most unhappy marriages reported the most dramatic turnarounds: among those who rated their marriages as very unhappy, almost eight out of 10 who avoided divorce were happily married five years later."[79] Dr. Waite and her associates used a nationally representative survey that analyzed 5,232 married persons in the late 1980s. Of those individuals, 645 rated their marriages as unhappy. The researchers followed these 645 persons for five years and again asked them to rate their personal happiness.

When these persons were reinterviewed, some had divorced, some were separated, and some were still married to the same person. The research yielded the following conclusions:

---

78 Linda J. Waite et. al., "Does Divorce Make People Happy?" Institute for American Values, https://docs.google.com/viewer?url=http://americanvalues.org/catalog/pdfs/does_divorce_make_people_happy.pdf.
79 Ibid.

- "Unhappily married adults who divorced or separated were no happier, on average, than unhappily married adults who stayed married. Even unhappy spouses who had divorced and remarried were no happier, on average, than unhappy spouses who stayed married.
- "Divorce did not reduce symptoms of depression for unhappily married adults, or raise their self-esteem, or increase their sense of mastery, on average, compared to unhappy spouses who stayed married.
- "The vast majority of divorces (74 percent) happened to adults who had been happily married five years previously. In this group, divorce was associated with dramatic declines in happiness and psychological well-being compared to those who stayed married.
- "Unhappy marriages were less common than unhappy spouses. Three out of four unhappily married adults were married to someone who was happy with the marriage.
- "Staying married did not typically trap unhappy spouses in violent relationships. Eighty-six percent of unhappily married adults reported no violence in their relationship (including 77 percent of unhappy spouses who later divorced or separated). Ninety-three percent of unhappy spouses who avoided divorce reported no violence in their marriage five years later.
- "Two out of three unhappily married adults who avoided divorce or separation ended up happily married five years later. Just one out of five unhappy spouses who divorced or separated had happily remarried in the same time period. Does this mean that most unhappy spouses who divorced would have ended up happily married if they had stuck with their marriages? We cannot say for sure."

After these findings, the team "conducted focus-group interviews with fifty-five marriage survivors—formerly unhappy husbands and wives who had turned their marriages around." Among other data they concluded the following:

> Many currently happily married spouses have had extended periods of marital unhappiness, often for quite serious reasons—alcoholism, infidelity, verbal abuse, emotional neglect, depression, illness, and work reversals. Why did these marriages survive where other marriages did not?

The *marital endurance ethic* appears to play a big role. Many spouses said that their "marriages got happier, not because they and their partner resolved problems, but because they stubbornly outlasted them. With time, these spouses said many sources of conflict and distress eased.

These spouses "typically had a low opinion of the benefits of divorce and had friends and family members who supported the importance of staying married."

The summary concluded, "We could find no evidence that divorce or separation typically made adults happier than staying in an unhappy marriage. Two out of three unhappily married adults who avoided divorce reported being happily married five years later."

One of the reasons divorce doesn't make life happier is because it has a major effect on the bank account. Recent research (May 2011) by the Family Research Council states, "Divorcing or separating mothers are 2.83 times more likely to be in poverty than those who remain married. Following a divorce, the parent with custody of the children experiences a 52 percent drop in his or her family income."[80]

Do these statistics mean that no one should get divorced or that all marriages, if they last long enough, will eventually be happy? No to both questions. But it *does* mean that marriage is something to believe in and to fight for. When a marriage is saved, it is a momentous accomplishment not only for the couple but also for their children and grandchildren, and for society in general.

Before applying for divorce, consider applying the Golden Rule. Try politeness, compassion, patience, repenting, forgiving, and enduring.

In horseback riding there is a kind of saddle known as an endurance saddle. If you don't know much about horseback riding, you may think that an endurance saddle helps the rider endure with less jolting and more comfort. In that assumption, you would be wrong. An endurance saddle helps the horse. The saddle is very lightweight and spreads the rider's weight more evenly over the horse's back. The phrase *"marital endurance"* similarly describes the idea that a husband and wife can find ways to make the marriage ride easier. Whenever possible, work to make your spouse's marriage better. Help your spouse endure being married to you; make the ride smoother.

---

80 Patrick F. Fagan, Andrew J. Kidd, and Henry Potrykus, "Marriage and Economic Well Being: The Economy of the Family Rises or Falls with Marriage," Marri Research, http://marri.us/get.cfm?i=RS11E03.

One husband who discovered this fact for himself said, "Happy wife—happy life."

A wife's version could be, "Happy husband—happy loved one," or "Happy he—happy me." Or for both husband and wife: "Happy spouse—happy house!"

Chapter 47

FAITH

FAITH IS THE FIRST PRINCIPLE of the gospel, something you've known since you learned the first Article of Faith. But faith's complexities aren't understood by memorizing eighteen words. Neither can you show a picture and say, "See. This is how faith looks." You can't play a song and say, "Listen. This is how faith sounds." Faith can't be seen, heard, smelled, touched, or tasted. Faith seems intangible, yet the Apostle Paul defined faith as a "substance" with "evidence"—"Now faith is the substance of things hoped for, the evidence of things not seen" (Hebrews 11:1). Even with that definition and after reading Ether 12, Hebrews 1, the Bible Dictionary, and *Lectures on Faith,* faith may remain intangible.

Perhaps defining what faith is *not* will illuminate what faith *is*. First, faith is not fear.

Moses experienced faith and fear. His faith allowed him to have a face-to-face conversation with God, which yielded pure knowledge. While in God's presence, Moses learned he was a son of God and saw that he was created in the image of God. He beheld a glorious vision of the world "and greatly marveled and wondered" (Moses 1:8). When the vision closed, "the presence of God withdrew from Moses, that his glory was not upon Moses; and Moses was left unto himself" (Moses 1:9).

Then "Satan came tempting him, saying: Moses, son of man, worship me. . . . Moses looked upon Satan and said: Who art thou? For behold, I am a son of God, in the similitude of his Only Begotten; and where is thy glory, that I should worship thee? For behold, I could not look upon God, except his glory should come upon me . . . But I can look upon thee in the natural man" (Moses 1:12–14). Satan reacted violently to this comparison and ranted in a loud, angry voice, commanding Moses to worship him. Then "Moses began to *fear* exceedingly; and as he began to *fear*, he saw the bitterness of hell" (Moses 1:20, emphasis added). Moses learned for himself the difference between faith and fear, between holy and unholy, between heavenly and hellish.

Faith is a gift from God that comes to those who ask for it and seek to do God's will. Fear opposes faith, but faith overcomes fear. They cannot coexist. "Fear not" is a common phrase in scripture.

"Fear not, Abram" (Genesis 15:1). "Fear not, [Hagar]" (Genesis 21:17). "Fear not, [Isaac]" (Genesis 26:24). "Fear not, [Jacob]" (Genesis 46:3). "Fear not, [Joshua]" (Joshua 8:1). "Fear not, [Isaiah]" (Isaiah 41:13). "Fear not, Mary" (Luke 1:30). "Fear not, Zacharias" (Luke 1:13). "Joseph, . . . Fear not" (Matthew 1:20). "Fear not, [shepherds]" (Luke 2:10). "Fear not, [Joseph Smith and Oliver Cowdery]" (D&C 6:33–36).

The scriptures provide reasons to "fear not." "I am thy shield" (Genesis 15:1). "I am with thee" (Genesis 26:24). "Thou hast found favor with God" (Luke 1:30). "I bring you good tidings of great joy" (Luke 2:10). "God will deliver" (Alma 61:21). "For they that be with us are more than they that be with them" (2 Kings 6:16).

Doubting is a type of fear. Four times in scripture the Lord says, "doubt not" (see Matthew 21:21, Mormon 9:27, D&C 6:36, and D&C 8:8).

Have you ever felt doubt sitting on your shoulder? Have you ever let one doubt in the door and discovered that ten sneak in? Doubt puts you on the threshold of fear. Doubt and fear cloud reason, and the more you doubt, the more you fear. Doubt and fear also disrupt the wavelength of the still, small voice of the Holy Ghost. One woman told of temptations that sat on her shoulder and whispered in her ear. At one point, she grew weary of the negative, seductive voice. She swiped her hand across her shoulder as to knock him off and said, "Leave me alone. I am not going to listen." Her dismissal of the unwelcome voice dismissed the fear and emptied her heart of doubt. In doing this, she opened her heart to promptings, reassurances, and ideas from the Holy Ghost. This is faith!

Church history is full of evidences of people who doubted not and moved forward in faith. Emer and Parna Harris were driven out of Missouri in 1839. Mobs were detaining individuals and searching for copies of the Book of Mormon. When one was found, the owner was tied to a tree and whipped, and the book was burned. Emer and Parna were determined to save some copies of the Book of Mormon. Emer, a skilled carpenter, created a false bottom in an old chest, placed copies in the secret compartment, filled the chest with their meager belongings, and proceeded on their journey.

Parna was walking in the lead when she was met by a mob of about four hundred men on horseback. The captain said to her: "Madam, are you a Mormon?"

She answered, "Yes, and I thank God for it."

The captain said, "We will have to search your wagon."

She replied, "You have driven us around so much I think you will find nothing but rags."

In searching the chest, they missed the false bottom and left the books undisturbed.[81] Parna exhibited her faith and feared "not what man [could] do" (Moroni 8:16).

Thomas David Evans, who was born in Wales, lost his leg below the knee in an accident when he was nine. As an adult, he came in contact with Mormon missionaries; joined the Church; came to America; pulled a handcart across the plains, walking on his wooden leg; and returned to Wales as a missionary twice. His wife, Priscilla, wrote:

> My husband had lost a leg in early childhood and walked on a wooden stump, which cause him a great deal of pain and discomfort. When his knee, which rested on a pad, became so very sore, my husband was not able to walk any farther, and I could not pull him in the little cart, being so sick myself [she was newly pregnant]. One late afternoon he felt he could not go on, so he stopped to rest beside some tall sagebrush. I pleaded with him to try to walk further, that if he stayed there he would die, and I could not go on without him. The company did not miss us until they rested for the night and when the names were checked we were not among the company. A rider on horse came back looking for us. When they saw the pitiful condition of my husband's knee, he was assigned to the commissary wagon [so he could ride] and helped dispense the food for the rest of the journey.[82]

In his journal, David speaks of crossing the plains with no mention of his leg. He tells of a couple times during one of his missions when his wooden leg made his travel difficult, but his journal is filled with

---

81 See http://harrisfamilynews.com/Stories_harris.htm.
82 Kate B. Carter, *Heart Throbs of the West*, 6:355.

accounts of faith. "One time when my companion . . . and I were in Pembrokeshire, a mob got after us and marched us out of town to the music of pans, horns, and bad eggs. They stood on the bridge and held me by the hair of the head over the water and threatened to throw me in if I did not deny that Joseph Smith was a prophet. I always felt to trust in the Lord while doing His work. They were the frightened ones when a large man walked into the crowd, and they scattered. When I turned to look for the man to thank him, he was nowhere to be seen."[83]

In the case of these pioneer forebears, we can almost see, hear, and feel the substance and evidence of their faith. In times of trial, they doubted not and as a result feared not. They believed the Lord, who said, "Fear thou not; for I am with thee: be not dismayed" (Isaiah 41:10). Faith is a magnet, drawing you to your Heavenly Father, and Him to you.

---

83 Journal of Thomas D. Evans, http://toastsandtidbits.blogspot.com/2009/04/my-great-great-great-grandfather-thomas.html.

Chapter 48

HOPE

DO YOU THINK OF HOPE as a junior faith, definitely less important? The Apostle Paul said that of faith, hope, and charity, charity is the greatest. So where does that leave hope? Is it hopelessly scrunched in the middle of *faithhopeandcharity*—as though it were a conjunction between faith and charity?

Hope is a powerful principle of purposeful living. Hope, even all by itself, changes lives. Hope is not the weak sister in the middle. The word the Apostle Peter used to define hope is "lively" (1 Peter 1:3). The footnote clarifies *lively* as *living*. Hope is a lively, living principle of the gospel. The prophet Moroni provides an additional view of hope by defining its opposite. "And if ye have no hope ye must needs be in despair" (Moroni 10:22). Previously, we spoke of fear and faith as opposites; now despair and hope are presented as opposites. Despair is everything negative; hope is everything positive.

A stake recently made a video of their youth explaining different principles of the gospel. Their expressions were deep and profound on every subject—except hope. When asked to define hope, one said, "Well, hope is, well, just hope. Like you hope you will do well on a test." Another said, "Hope is when you feel alone and hope someone will call or text you." In these examples *hope* is more like a synonym for *wish*. We use *hope* this way ourselves. "I *hope* I don't get caught in traffic." "I *hope* I don't have to have a root canal." "I *hope* my favorite team wins the game."

True hope, the principle of the gospel, is like faith in that it is not just *hope* but rather *hope* in Jesus Christ. We learn this from the fourth Article of Faith. "We believe the first principles and ordinances of the gospel are first, Faith—" Not just faith, but "faith in the Lord Jesus Christ." The same applies to *hope*. Hope is just not any old hope. To be more than wishing and to be effectual, hope must be in the Lord Jesus Christ.

Joseph Smith taught that faith is a principle of both action and power (see *Lectures on Faith,* 3). Likewise, hope is a vibrant, living, positive principle of the gospel that leads to righteous actions. Hope anticipates good in the future. Hope expresses a worthwhile desire. Hope can exist when there is nothing else. Hope takes perseverance and patience, and it expects positive outcomes. Hope takes your faith and projects it into the future.

When I found a lump in my breast, I hoped it would go away. When it didn't, I hoped it would not be malignant. When it was malignant, I hoped it wouldn't be in the lymph nodes. When it was in the lymph nodes, I hoped the cancer hadn't metastasized. When it hadn't, I switched to hoping my hair wouldn't fall out during chemotherapy. When my hair did fall out, I hoped it would grow back in. Cancer taught me to hope, hope, and hope again.

When I received my cancer diagnosis, I knew I had a choice—to be in a constant state of despair or to feel the power of hope. I learned a new hope can be born every second. When there is nothing else, there is always hope. Faith and hope are linked like two sisters walking arm in arm.

Hope is a gift of the Spirit. James 1:5–6 explains the process required to receive spiritual gifts. "If any of you lack ___, let him ask of God." That's the pattern. Just fill in the blank with a virtue or gift of the Spirit you desire. "If any of you lack [hope or patience or discernment or charity], "let him ask of God that giveth to all men liberally, and upbraideth not; and it shall be given him. But let him ask in faith, nothing wavering."

Hope is the painting you have in your mind of what your future looks like. If you can't envision it, how can you work toward it? Visualizing your hopes is the key for a better future—the very next minute and decades beyond. Hope is Heavenly Father's great plan of happiness for you. Moroni instructed, "Whoso believeth in God might with surety hope for a better world" (Ether 12:4). This is a promise. You believe in God; consequently, you can hope with surety. What does he mean *with surety*? Moroni is issuing a guarantee. Hope produces men and women with limitless potential—guaranteed.

Hope in Jesus Christ is a potent principle with powerful promise, not a subset of faith, not a conjunction squished between faith and charity. Hope for hope, pray for the gift of hope, and live in *lively* hope.

Chapter 49

AND CHARITY

THE RELIEF SOCIETY OF THE Church of Jesus Christ of Latter-day Saints was organized more than 170 years ago and is now the largest women's organization in the world. The motto of Relief Society is "Charity Never Faileth."

Do you believe the motto is true? Have your attempts at charity ever failed? When your charitable efforts backfire, do you think the lofty-sounding motto states an ideal and is not attainable?

Never is such a bold choice of a word. It is so restrictive. Never means never in the past and never in the future. Not once can charity have failed for the motto to be true.

The Apostle Paul wrote those three words in a letter to the Corinthians (see 1 Corinthians 13:8), and the prophet Mormon wrote the same words in a letter to his son Moroni (see Moroni 7:46). Both men link charity with faith and hope, stating that of the three, charity is the greatest. They aren't talking of *a* charity, an organization to help the poor. The prophet Alma explained, "See that ye have faith, and charity, and then ye will always abound in good works" (Alma 7:24). Here we come to understand that charity is something you are, something you have, but we are again confronted with another absolute. *Always* is every single time.

In Lamentations 3:22–23, we read, "The Lord's . . . compassions fail not. They are new every morning." How beautiful! Every morning there is a new supply of the Lord's compassions, and He *never* runs out of them! Is not "His compassions fail not" another way of saying "Charity never faileth"?

"Give ear, O earth, and rejoice ye inhabitants thereof, for the Lord is God. . . . His purposes fail not" (D&C 76:1–3). "His purposes fail not" again claims that charity is indeed fail-proof.

In other scriptures we discover "that the mouths of the prophets shall not fail" (D&C 58:8), which validates the words of both Paul and Mormon. Then Jesus Christ himself said, "My words are sure and shall not fail" (D&C 64:31).

And herein lies the verification that "Charity never faileth." It is because charity is first and only about Jesus Christ. *He* is the reason and definition of charity. Charity never fails because Christ will not fail. Charity equals Christ.

Both Paul and Mormon defined "charity" by describing Jesus Christ. If we change "*charity*" to "*Christ*" in Mormon's words, the intent of the verses becomes clearer: "And *Christ* suffereth long, and is kind, envieth not, and is not puffed up, seeketh not *His* own, is not easily provoked, thinketh no evil, and rejoiceth not in iniquity but rejoiceth in the truth, beareth all things, believeth all things, hopeth all things, endureth all things. Wherefore, my beloved [sisters], if ye have not *Christ*, ye are nothing, for *Christ* never faileth. Wherefore, cleave unto *Christ*, who is the greatest of all, for all things must fail—But *Christ*" (Moroni 7:45–47). *Everything* else fails.

The Apostle Paul said that even if you speak like an angel, even if you have the gift of prophecy, even if you understand all mysteries, even if you have all knowledge and all faith, even if you give all your possessions to the poor, it profits you nothing. It only counts if you have charity—love of, like, and for Jesus Christ (see 1 Corinthians 13:2). Charity is not just doing good but rather loving others as purely as Jesus Christ loves.

Charity is not something you *earn*; it is a spiritual gift you *receive*. Mormon explained that you acquire this precious gift by asking for it in prayer. "Wherefore, my beloved [sisters], pray unto the Father." This can't be a prayer you dash off with a few quick words and expect the gift of charity to be yours. You are asking to be different than you are. You are asking to be better than you are. You are asking not for a temporary feeling of love and compassion but for a change of heart, even a new heart. "A new heart also will I give you, and a new spirit will I put within you: and I will take away the stony heart out of your flesh, and I will give you an heart of flesh" (Ezekiel 36:26).

Charity will become who and what you are, as real and tangible as if you were wearing a cloak or a shawl. "And above all things, clothe yourselves with the bond of charity, as with a mantle" (D&C 88:125).

As we learn, experience, and grow through the Spirit's tutoring, as we pray "with all the energy of heart," the promised gift, this pure love of Christ, will be conferred on us. Clothed in charity we will feel His compassion, His mercy, His purposes, His charity. "Wherefore, cleave unto charity" (Moroni 7:46).

Chapter 50

THE WAY HOME

"THEN ONE OF THEM . . . asked him a question . . . saying, Master, which is the great commandment in the law? Jesus said unto him, Thou shalt love the Lord thy God with all thy heart, and with all thy soul, and with all thy mind. This is the first and great commandment" (Matthew 22:35–38).

At face value, this commandment seems impossible because it is not measureable. To love God to the extent required—with all thy heart, soul, and mind—is overwhelming. Yet, a commandment wouldn't be given, especially the first and great commandment, if it were not possible.

Joseph Smith said, "It is the first principle of the gospel to know for a certainty the character of God."[84] "For a certainty" means to know God's character because if you love a God who doesn't exist, you are like a child waiting for Santa Claus. You can't love Him if you don't know Him. Your energy and desire are wasted. However, if your energies and desires are to love and serve "the only true God" (John 17:3), you spend your life in that humble quest.

If it's that simple, why are there so many "versions" of God out there in the world? Why is knowing God such a confused subject? Please consider this possibility: if you were the devil, would not your top priority be to confuse people about the most important subject in the world? Satan does not want us to know or understand God because, as Joseph Smith said, "When we understand the character of God, and know how to come to Him, he begins to unfold the heavens to us, and to tell us all about it."[85]

---

84 Joseph Smith, B. H. Roberts, *History of the Church*, Salt Lake City: Deseret Book Company, 1912, 6:305.
85 Ibid., 6:308.

Satan confuses and distorts, but Heavenly Father provides a way for His children to learn to know Him and cast away all worldly misperceptions and misrepresentations of Him. That way is to come to know the Father by learning about His Son. Jesus Christ announced, "The Son can do nothing of himself, but what he seeth the Father do: for what things whatsoever he doeth, these also doeth the Son likewise" (John 5:19). Jesus also taught, "The Father which sent me, he gave me a commandment, what I should say, and what I should speak" (John 12:49).

The words of Jesus Christ reveal His Father's purpose: "For behold, this is my work and my glory—to bring to pass the immortality and eternal life of man" (Moses 1:39).They show affection, "I love the Father" (John 14:31), and deference, "Holy Father . . . O righteous Father" (John 17:11, 25). "Our Father which art in heaven, hallowed be thy name" (Matthew 6:9).

Jesus Christ's words express gratitude: "Father, I thank thee that thou hast heard me" (John 11:41). They honor the Father: "For thine is the kingdom, and the power, and the glory, for ever" (Matthew 6:13). His actions illustrate humility: "For I do always those things that please him" (John 8:29). They bespeak fidelity: "The works which the Father hath given me to finish, the same works . . . I do" (John 5:36).

The words of Jesus Christ show absolute obedience: "I seek not mine own will, but the will of the Father which hath sent me" (John 5:30). His actions show absolute faith: "And he went a little further, and fell on his face, and prayed, saying, O my Father, if it be possible, let this cup pass from me: nevertheless not as I will, but as thou wilt" (Matthew 26:39).

Thus we learn from His Only Begotten Son how to come to know and love God. As we study the life of Jesus Christ, the character of God is unfolded and we internalize the truth: "And this is life eternal, that they might know thee the only true God, and Jesus Christ, whom thou hast sent" (John 17:3).

Whatever knowledge we begin to accumulate through our love and efforts comes line upon line, and this continues throughout eternity. Individual intelligence is blessed with light and comprehension as it is earned. How is it earned? By obeying the laws, the commandments, and the ordinances. This is the only way.[86] The simple law of heaven is that the most obedient receive the greatest understanding and knowledge.

---

86 See Bruce R. McConkie, *Doctrinal New Testament Commentary*, Salt Lake City: Deseret Book Company, 3:378.

The writer of the book of Jude illustrates how the way to eternal life is a polar-opposite from the empty and dark way of Satan. He said Satan's followers are like "clouds . . . without water . . . ; trees whose fruit withereth . . . raging waves of the sea, foaming out their own shame; wandering stars, to whom is reserved the blackness of darkness for ever" (1:12–13). The Apostle John said that if you are in that "blackness of darkness," though the light of the gospel may shine, "the darkness comprehend[s] it not" (John 1:5).

So why is the world so bewildered about the nature of God when the scriptures are so clear? The scriptures also answer that question. The world knows not God because of *cunning*. *Cunning* describes how Satan and his minions go about confusing, deceiving, and teaching false doctrine.

The Apostle Paul warned about "cunning craftiness" wherein men "lie in wait to deceive" (Ephesians 4:14). The prophet Jacob warned about "the cunning plan of the evil one" (2 Nephi 9:28). Alma warned that cunning men are "wise as to the wisdom of the world" (Alma 2:1). These are men who know "all the arts and cunning of the people" (Alma 10:15). Alma also warned of "the power of the devil, which comes by [his] cunning plans" (Alma 28:13). The Lord said there are and will be "evils and designs . . . in the hearts of conspiring [cunning] men" (D&C 89:4).

We overcome the cunning of the devil by following the prophets. By following the prophets, we are worthy of the companionship of the Holy Ghost. By following the promptings of the Holy Ghost, we are led to Jesus Christ. By following Jesus Christ, we come to know the character of God our Eternal Father. It is a divine plan of following the leader.

Our family had a party in a secluded canyon that is accessed via a dirt road with steep switchbacks. The party ended when it grew dark. Only a few family members remained to load the cars and put out the fires. With the fires out, it was very dark. Only a few stars lit the path. I was afraid to be the lead car down the dark canyon and asked my son, "May I follow you?" He kindly led the way to the mouth of the canyon, where there was a ranger station at which you had to pay a fee. He stopped at the fee station then waved good-bye to me out the window. When I stopped to pay, the ranger said, "The gentleman you were following paid for you."

In this way, we come to know God. We follow the Gentle Man, whose example we trust to lead us through the dark switchbacks of life.

In a future time, you will approach the gates of heaven. You will stop at a station and know there are requirements to be paid before you can proceed. You will look at the Keeper of the Gate and be privileged to recognize Him as the Gentle Man you have endeavored to follow. You will hear Him say, "Father, I paid for her."

About the Author

MARILYNNE ENJOYS THINKING AND WRITING about why women do the things we do and how the job of living can be happier. She believes the gospel of Jesus Christ is the key to happiness today and in a million years. Her most beautiful moments come when she is with any combination of family at home, playing word games or piano duets, visiting a Church or national historic site, walking on warm sandy beaches, or hiking the red rock canyons of Southern Utah. She has passion for history— American history, LDS Church history, and writing family histories. She knows that those who write about history make history because only those things that are recorded are remembered. As wife of Richard, mother of eight, mother-in-law of six, grandmother of twenty-three, and great-grandmother of Maggie, she has many opportunities to experience love and life. She is a breast cancer survivor of eighteen years. She has written ten other books and many articles in anthologies and magazines.